RAISING MEN

RAISING
MEN

**Lessons Navy SEALs Learned from
Their Training and Taught to Their Sons**

ERIC DAVIS
with Dina Santorelli

St. Martin's Press
New York

www.stmartins.com

Library of Congress Cataloging-in-Publication Data

First Edition: May 2016
Names: Davis, Eric, 1972– author.
Title: Raising men : lessons Navy SEALs learned from their training and taught to their sons / Eric Davis.
Other titles: Lessons Navy SEALs learned from their training and taught to their sons
Description: First edition. | New York : St. Martin's Press, [2016]
Identifiers: LCCN 2016003975| ISBN 9781250091734 (hardcover) | ISBN 9781250091741 (e-book)
Subjects: LCSH: Davis, Eric, 1972– | United States. Navy. SEALs—Officers—Biography. | United States. Navy. SEALs—Training of—Anecdotes. | Parenting. | Fathers and sons—United States. | Physical fitness for children—Anecdotes. | Discipline of children—Anecdotes. | Character in children—Anecdotes. | Mental toughness—Anecdotes. | Conduct of life.
Classification: LCC VG87 .D385 2016 | DDC 650.1—dc23
LC record available at http://lccn.loc.gov/2016003975

Our books may be purchased in bulk for promotional, educational, or business use. Please contact your local bookseller or the Macmillan Corporate and Premium Sales Department at 1-800-221-7945, extension 5442, or by e-mail at MacmillanSpecialMarkets@macmillan.com.

First Edition: May 2016

10   9   8   7   6   5   4   3   2   1

Table of Confidence

Author's Note

The stories in this book about SEALs and their sons are true. However, some names and details have been changed. In particular, no SEAL has been named or identified without his express approval.

Because of my special training, application of SEAL principles to my parenting has at times involved situations that might be dangerous for the average child or father. Readers should, of course, not attempt to duplicate activities that would be dangerous for them, and they should apply common sense in assessing their capacity to follow, or as necessary to modify, the lessons presented in this book.

RAISING
MEN

INTRODUCTION

Do It on Purpose

Sweating and dehydrated in the hot desert of Niland, California, I had two hours left on this last stalk, and if I didn't pass, I would be dropped from sniper school.

I had already been on my belly crawling for hours—toward the wrong target. After spending four weeks, six hours a day, in the desert, I still hadn't mastered the art of stalking my target. Somehow through instinct, luck, and sheer will I made it to my final firing position (FFP) with five minutes left to build and take my shot when suddenly I heard—

"Freeze!"

It was the sound that every sniper student dreaded: An instructor in the observation post (OP) had spotted a student in the field. *Was it me? Was I out in the open? Did I shake a tree?* Several minutes went by. A walker, or field instructor, passed within inches of me. I choked down some half-dry saliva and sand resting in the back of my throat, expecting to hear the sniper-career-ending words "Sniper at your feet!"

"Stay lower," the walker whispered mercifully instead. "I

think they can see anything above my knee." He walked away toward the crackle of a radio from the other side of the field. I was still safe.

I remained perfectly still. This exercise was all about being stealthy, about getting your simulated shots off while under intense observation. The objective was to take two shots—the first while you were in your FFP and not under direct observation, and the second as the walker worked you, which meant he got within 10 yards of you, allowing the instructors in the OP to watch you as you chambered and shot the second blank. They wanted to evaluate your muzzle blast to see if there would be dust or leaves flying up. A Navy SEAL sniper was expected to be invisible while he was firing—even when someone was looking right at him with the best binoculars that money could buy.

With only two minutes left to do what normally takes between thirty minutes and two hours, I got in position to take my shots. Hoping the instructor's gaze had moved away, I chambered my round, took a deep breath, and sprinted to a nearby tree. Standing out like a set of dog's balls and with time ticking down, I abandoned all strategies of stealth and counted on luck as I dove barrel-first into the tree—

Bang!

I shot my first round just before the timer went off and thought, *Oh, shit. I just failed sniper school.* (The rules say that once you take your first shot, you can't move or do anything to improve your position, and my position needed some major improvement.) I waited perfectly still for the walker to work me. After signaling the instructors in the OP to look my way, he said, "Shot in three, two, one, fire!" and I took my second shot.

Click.

Nothing happened.

Shit, I thought, *I had a dud.*

I'd have to find and chamber another round while they were watching, which, if I had brought another round, might not have been so bad.

"Well, I guess you're going to have to try that one again. I hope it works, brother," the walker said, more as a teammate than as my instructor.

I rechambered the dud blank and recycled the bolt of my Remington 700. When the sound of the gunfire settled, the walker confirmed I was within the proper distance of my target, 180 to 220 yards, and then said the words that, to this day, I still cannot believe: "You passed."

CHASING THE BULL

Becoming a father is not much different than becoming a sniper. It's hard, not a lot of guys can easily pull it off, and it requires incredible amounts of patience, discipline, and focus. We're out in front trying to locate, stalk, and take down high-value targets to protect what's ours while under direct observation and criticism— from spouses, kids, other parents, society. We crawl for days, or years, trying to make forward progress, leading our families through unknown territory as we figure things out for ourselves, depending on luck and a whole lot of mercy to achieve our objectives.

There was a phrase I used as a sniper instructor to explain to my students what was preventing them from consistently hitting their targets. I called it *chasing the bull* ("bull" is short for bull's-eye): They would continually rely on what seemed obvious and intuitive to make their shot without ever considering the possibility that the source of their problem might lie elsewhere. Many factors affect a sniper's ability to successfully and reliably nail a target. The most obvious is his *scope,* the magnifying optic with embedded crosshairs mounted on the top of his rifle: Turn the knob five clicks to the right, move the impact of your bullet five inches to the left. Easy. However, scopes are rarely what cause snipers to miss. Many times, the source of the trouble is less obvious. Wind, lighting, humidity, body position, trigger squeeze, air density, angles, body alignment, respirations, and even the rotation of the earth can become factors.

These elements often get missed or ignored because on their own they have a limited impact on the accuracy of a shot; however, together, they can—and do—add up to a complete miss. Making learning even more difficult is that many of these factors change moment by moment. I once saw a sniper in training attempt to take a head shot from 800 yards away and, because of some downrange wind, miss to the right. He then readjusted his scope to the left, because he assumed it was incorrectly set rather than considering the possibility that he had misread or missed the wind. When he took his next shot, the previously unnoticed wind had stopped, and he fired and missed to the left. To him, unaware of the hidden force of the wind, it felt like there was something wrong with his gun. (Hell, you can miss an 800-yard head shot because you ate spicy food for lunch.)

And so begins the chase. Replace the scope, replace the gun, and nothing changes, or some shots hit and some shots miss. Many students have failed out of sniper school not because they were incapable of performing the tasks required, or because their equipment was faulty, but because they were unable to see beyond their current intuition and understanding. The concept that the direction of the sun coupled with the position of their body could cause them to miss a target today that they drilled yesterday was beyond them. Therefore, the cause of their failure remained hidden. They'd have no recourse but to chase the bull.

As fathers we face the same challenges of sometimes hitting our targets and sometimes not. We rely on what we were taught by our own fathers or count on our intuition and cultural norms to pull us through, and when we get stuck or fail, we cycle through the solutions with which we're most familiar and comfortable. We stick to what we know without considering what we don't know.

I've seen too many fathers experience high levels of shame, doubt, frustration, and failure for two main reasons:

+ They mistakenly adopt their father's, or family's, cultural assumptions about manhood, choosing a firm, authoritarian style of parenting that relies on harsh discipline, coercive punishment, and the restriction of love.

+ Due to apathy, laziness, or busyness, they crank the knob on their fathering scope so far in the other direction that they cripple their son's ability to grow—either by giving him everything he wants or by insulating him from the natural and necessary consequences of his choices and behaviors, which denies him the opportunity to learn and grow. It's like they lift their sons up and over the very obstacle course that is meant to develop the strength and skill that they need to survive and thrive.

Both groups are not able to see beyond their existing knowledge to understand the real factors taking them out. Because of the high-threat environment in which SEALs operate, they work hard to discover and learn these underlying principles, which affect their ability to survive and dominate out in the field. Because people's lives are on the line, they learn not to chase the bull, but to do the hard work and to correct the problem—with no excuses. Many parents don't realize that the actions and abilities they embody are a matter of life and death, just as much as they are on a typical SEAL mission. The consequences may not be immediate, but they can be just as fatal.

What It Takes to Be a SEAL Parent

+ Courage
+ Respect
+ Honor
+ Perseverance
+ Innovation
+ Communication
+ Confidence
+ Responsibility

HERE'S WHAT I GOT

The U.S. Navy's Sea, Air, and Land Teams, known as the Navy SEALs, have become the premier Special Operations force of the United States. Currently, there are approximately 2,500 active Navy SEALs, representing less than 1 percent of all navy personnel.

I served as a Navy SEAL from 1998 to 2008, stationed in Coronado, California. I deployed on four separate occasions and executed more than thirty successful missions, many of them requiring me to pirate ships in the Middle East, and others requiring me to perform intelligence work in unnamed places. I am honored to be a decorated veteran of the Global War on Terror and was lucky enough to become proficient in the art of technical and physical surveillance, allowing me to be hand-selected to perform intelligence collections in denied areas around the world. I was also fortunate enough to serve as a sniper instructor for half of my time in the SEAL Teams, during which I had the honor of training men such as Marcus Luttrell and Chris Kyle.

One of my best friends, former Navy SEAL Brandon Webb, and I went through BUD/S, served at SEAL Team 3, and taught snipers together during our careers. (If you read his book *Red Circle,* you may be able to pick up on his subtle recognition of how I carried him through each phase of our careers.) Together and under one of the most amazing leaders I've ever worked for, Master Chief "M," Brandon and I, and the other sniper instructors, were able to significantly reduce the failure rate of Naval Special Warfare's internationally recognized sniper course—the course had been so difficult to pass that experienced Special Forces Operators would fail regularly. (Every SEAL platoon is required to have a certain number of qualified snipers on it to be deployable.) During our tenure, the attrition rate plummeted from the double digits to just 5 percent, and we accomplished this without additional money or time, and without lowering our standards. This success was all in relation to performance through process, passion, and principles—exactly, as you'll read, what this book is about.

Since departing from the SEAL Teams in 2008, I've been repurposing and delivering the proven principles of performance used by the Teams for both organizations and individuals. I've used these principles to redesign and deploy corporate sales programs as well as individual performance initiatives. I also use them in my own life as a successful father, husband, entrepreneur, and writer.

TRUE ACTION vs. USELESS MOVEMENT

For a SEAL, every action has a purpose, every mission has an objective. However, in the civilian world, few people truly understand the meaning or purpose of action, which is why so many find themselves stuck—in their careers, in their projects, or in their relationships with their significant others or their children. There is one key difference between action and movement:

Action: Effort, with a meaningful objective.

Movement: Effort.

Movement simply makes you *feel* like you're doing something or getting somewhere. It is busyness and effort without progress. It's not even like stalking the wrong target. It's like stalking *no* target—head down, brutally crawling nowhere. Ask yourself:

+ What three things do you spend time and/or energy on every day that are meaningless? What activities could you stop doing right now and your life would be just fine?

+ What are three objectives that you spend time and energy on every day that are meaningful? What activities greatly impact, in a positive way, your ability to parent?

Fundamentally, performance in every domain shares common principles. Concepts such as strategy, leadership, and team building are as applicable to a SEAL Team as they are to a sniper team, a sales team, or a parenting team; the missions may vary, but the requirements are the same. At the core of success for every father, sniper, or CEO is the ability to recognize, master, and manage the underlying factors that affect each and every tactic, person, and situation he encounters. When these underlying factors are not recognized and dealt with, there's nothing left to do but chase the bull.

OUR BOYS NEED OUR HELP

I have four children: three daughters—Taylor, twenty-three; Ella, eleven; and Lea, nine—and one son, Jason, twenty. They're not always perfect, but they are drug-free, self-confident, respectful toward others, and, most important, happy. I treat them equally. I parent them with the same principles. However, there's a reason why I've chosen to focus on boys, on raising men, for this book.

I see far too many dudes getting their asses handed to them— they're stuck in the wrong careers, not making enough money, not healthy or active, or just plain miserable. For generations, fathers have been slowly slipping out of the parenting game. When the Industrial Revolution hit, we headed away from our homes to make the almighty dollar, and for many years our success as a father was measured solely by our financial contributions—our ability to make a lot of money for our family. Tradition, heritage, and the art of manhood stopped being passed down and transferred to our sons, because we were straight-up too busy punching the clock. Our absence allowed our manhood to get shoved around and redefined by others and by popular culture. While the sheepdogs were away, the punks played.

We must reclaim our role. We must lead by example. How can we expect our boys to become powerful, successful, and complete

THIS MEANS WAR

Parenting kicks your ass, but, like war, it propels you to innovate and operate with high levels of excellence and efficiency. In the military, there are two types of warfare:

+ **Symmetrical warfare:** The two opposing sides have similar and conventional military power, resources, and tactics. It's basically force on force. Not a lot of variety. Think of the schoolbook images of Redcoats standing on a hill and shooting at a group of Whitecoats who are doing the same. Winning comes down to which side is the largest or which side works the hardest. This requires little training or skill.

+ **Asymmetrical warfare:** The opposing sides differ greatly in size, morals, codes of conduct, tactics, and strategies. If you've ever seen the movie *The Patriot*, you'll notice that the lead character, Benjamin Martin, played by Mel Gibson, bends over the larger British force with a small element of colonials by abandoning the manners of war and resorting to what is considered unconventional warfare—camouflage and concealment, deception, and covert and clandestine operations. It's how you win. This requires a lot of training, skill, and innovation. Principles must be understood.

Think of parenting as asymmetrical and unconventional warfare. Any and every discourse can and is used to wage war—drugs, alcohol, peer pressure, texting, advertising, social media. The variations of attack are endless, and the only way to win is to become whatever is needed or expected of you. Being a father in this day and age is a thinking man's game. We must learn to become an expert at becoming an expert.

men if we ourselves don't possess or act on the tools and the know-how to take them there? This book is as much about us being a man as it is about our sons becoming one.

In today's dynamic and high-threat world, a new type of father must prevail. We have to go beyond the duties of the traditional breadwinner. Our sons need us to be part of the family—to lead, to love, and to teach them the ways of the world, outside and inside our front door. Men, we need to square ourselves away, or else we will fail our sons—and ourselves—by falling short and leaving them hanging.

I know there's a lot of bullshit out there, and we've all become jaded when it comes to self-help books and all those pink- and blue-covered parenting books littering bookstores. This book is not that. I've spent a lifetime searching for answers about manhood and fathering, and nothing I've seen has proven to be as sound and reliable as the principles that the men of the SEAL Teams and other Special Operations forces have been leveraging and exploiting for years.

I've organized this book around a series of fundamental and powerful SEAL training principles, repurposing them for fatherhood, so that you, too, can discover those mysterious factors that seem to thwart your every fathering move. I've invited a group of my SEAL brothers, some of the finest examples of men I know, to share their parenting stories as well. Navy SEALs may not be parenting experts, but they *are* experts at getting the job done. They kick ass and raise kids in ways that have opened my eyes and will open yours. You'll also hear from my wife, Belisa, and my son, Jason, to find out what impact they think the SEAL principles have had on our family.

CLEAR END STATES

A large part of being a leader is the ability to define and communicate what SEALs call *clear end states*. These are the conditions and criteria of a final objective—how things will look and feel when you get there—within any given category of performance. By defining these end states, you'll be able to strategize and focus all of your effort and energy toward a more productive future for you and your son.

At the end of each chapter is a Debrief, a series of questions that will offer you an opportunity to start building your personal parenting mission statement. Don't worry about making a project out of them or sharing them with your spouse or even writing anything down for now. Just use the space to consider how these core end states will help shape the role you, as a father, must systematically pursue and nail.

EXTREME PARENTING?

A SEAL's approach to being a father can seem a bit extreme, especially when I talk about tying the hands and legs of my kids together and throwing them into a pool (chapter 2), but it's often through extreme experiences that we learn the most about ourselves and about what's important. I'm not saying that you *need* to throw your kid off a cliff or into a pool in order to be a good father. That's not the point. The point is to show you what I do, to exaggerate the example, so that you can see the principles behind my actions—the life fundamentals that are often hidden and subtle. My hope is to help you uncover the kind of things that are so human and deep within us that once you understand them, you'll wonder why you've never noticed them before.

This technique of using the extreme to reveal the subtle is something I developed as a sniper instructor. When students had a hard time understanding a concept, such as how wind could affect the impact of their bullets, I would encourage them to imagine the effect of shooting a beach ball instead of a bullet, and suddenly the effect of the wind was pretty obvious. That's what we're doing here, showcasing the extreme to demonstrate the basics. We want to help you to see what's going on, so that you can be a better father—not by working harder but by ceasing to chase the bull and redeploying your current time and energy to what really matters, in a way that really matters.

As fathers, our objective is to produce a bond and a relationship of honor, trust, and respect with our children so that we can guide them for the rest of their lives and help them make the choices that will allow them to succeed. This is how I do it. I'm a former Navy SEAL who went through some shit and came out on the other side with four great kids. Maybe the future will bring some new challenges, but the principles on which my children were raised and that are discussed in this book will help us through them. We all have our moments of weakness, but success—whether in the SEALs, in parenting, or in life—is about recognizing those moments so that we can recover and grow from them.

Whether you have a newborn, teenagers, or adult children, it's time to take control of your parenting and your mission objectives as they pertain to you and your kids. I was just barely nineteen years old when I brought home my daughter Taylor. I didn't know what I was getting into. I was emotionally, physically, and spiritually ill-prepared, not unlike when I was in BUD/S or sniper school, but somehow I knew that I would get fatherhood right. (It was so ingrained in me that I spent a drunken night in Singapore getting the Japanese kanji character meaning "father" tattooed on my back.) That's because it was an objective that I wanted, a path that I *chose,* like being a SEAL.

There's a great power in choice, and a great opportunity—to learn, to grow, to begin, or to begin again. There may not be a definitive word on being a man, or on raising one, but the shit I've learned in the SEAL Teams has taught me that you'll never find out what is in you until you are all in, so let's put it all on the table. The stakes are too high for us to "wing it" or depend on our intuition. Time is too short to chase the bull of fatherhood. Fellas, we've got a job to do. It's time to parent on purpose. It's time to do it right. It's time to take back what is ours and redefine an entire generation of men, starting with ourselves and our sons. It's time to get some.

As they say in the Teams: *Hooyah, motherfucker!*

1

BUILDING A TEAM

My class was already a few weeks into BUD/S (Basic Underwater Demolition/SEAL) when Instructor Samuels directed us into the First Phase classroom for a special brief. We shuffled in quickly but quietly, looking more like prisoners of war than SEAL trainees—heads down, our wet and sandy boots sliding rhythmically across the tiled floor.

As I made my way to one of the chairs—the kind they have in high school, with the desk attached to the side—a high-ranking SEAL officer was standing off in the corner of the room. My heart cramped a bit. I was certain his presence meant that we had fucked something up so bad that the level of hammering we were about to experience was to be so intense that it would require congressional oversight. People do *die* in SEAL training. Not very often, but it does happen. As we waited, our collective body heat evaporated the saltwater that had become a permanent part of our uniforms, since, in this early phase of training, it was routine for us to hit the surf so often that we never actually got to dry off. The room smelled like a harbor on a hot sunny day.

"You guys are steaming up my class," Instructor Samuels said quietly. "Go hit the surf and get back. You've got sixty-five seconds." He said it as if we should have already thought of it ourselves. He glanced down at his black G-Shock watch. *Ding.* His timer started.

Instantly, a hundred dudes cycled out of the classroom, across the SEAL compound, through the parking lot, over the sand berm, and into the salty ocean. We made it back in what had to be close to sixty-five seconds, but judging by Instructor Samuels's face, we had just stacked yet another failure that we'd no doubt pay for later.

Instructor Samuels, all 5' 11" and about 180 pounds of him, stood at the front of the room. He was like a young and extremely fit Richard Gere, but with a light southern accent. "To be honest, you guys aren't even worth talking to right now, because most of you will quit by the end of the week," he said in a straightforward yet friendly tone, "but Mr. Smith is heading off to Africa, so we had to push up his brief." He stepped aside, and Captain Smith crossed to the front of the room. He was shorter and leaner than Samuels, with a mustache, and looked more like a presidential candidate than a SEAL.

"How are you fellas doing?" Captain Smith asked, even though he knew the answer.

"*Hooyah,*" we responded collectively.

"So have you figured out what this is all about yet?" he asked.

This time, just a couple of guys answered, "*Hooyah,*" which meant *I don't know what you're talking about, but I felt like I just had to respond.*

Captain Smith and Instructor Samuels exchanged a *what a bunch of dumbasses* look, and then Captain Smith surprised me with what he said next.

"I'm here to explain why we are doing what we are doing to you."

This caught me off guard, considering the first part of our SEAL training was all balls to the wall, pedal to the metal, a *not for me to ask why but for me to do or die* type of thing. If the instructors said to dive into the cold ocean, you dove in and stayed there until you were hypothermic. If they said to carry your buddy on your shoulders, you carried him until you dropped, and then you kept crawling with him strung across your back. For them to stop and dial us in to what was going on was meaningful. I realized that they wanted us to be *thinkers* as well as doers—a paradigm shift from typical military training that would later change my life forever.

SEAL SPEAK

Hooyah: a form of release; an expression of mind over matter, of attitude and mental self-regulation. It has many meanings, but these three are among the most common: *Yes, I can do it; Right on;* and *You're a fucking cocksucker.*

BUD/S training consists of approximately six months of field training divided into three phases:

+ Basic Conditioning Phase: SEALs are taught to rely on themselves and the presence of others. Threat: You can inconvenience others and hurt yourself.
+ Combat Diving Phase: SEALs are taught to rely on themselves and their dive buddy. Threat: You can get your buddy kicked out of training or killed.
+ Land Warfare: SEALs are taught to rely on their team to produce nearly impossible results. Threat: You can kill the entire class.

READY TO LEAD. READY TO FOLLOW.
NEVER QUIT.

Do SEAL candidates ever quit? Yes, of course they do, up-wards of 70 percent of them. First Phase weeds out a lot of guys for a lot of reasons, but at the core of the matter, it's because of their inability to see past, or override, their personal preferences and desire for immediate comfort.

Do fathers ever quit? Yes, and I don't just mean that they walk away. I've heard the expression *Once a father, always a father,* but I've come across many dads who have thrown in the towel—it just doesn't *look* like quitting. My defini-tion of a father is someone who is there for his children, someone who spends a certain amount of time doing homework, having fun, and offering advice. By that defini-tion, a father who *chooses* to work too much or to spend the majority of his time hanging out with his friends or at the bar instead of spending time with his children is not really acting like a father. Has he quit? No, not officially. However, at his core, he quits every time he allows his personal preference and desire for immediate comfort to take him out of the game. Any father reading this knows what I'm talking about.

What about the father who is home all the time but would rather binge-watch television shows than play a game or go for a hike or a surf? Has he quit? No one's probably going to call him out on it, but he has. Instead of *being there,* he's just *there.* This is important because in SEAL training when a candidate quits, he is removed from training so that he can no longer do any damage to him-self or the class. However, when a father quits, he'll likely still be present in his children's lives and can inflict harm, particularly if he ignores his kids or damages their self-esteem and confidence by being emotionally removed from them.

The good news? If you've stepped out—of SEAL training or of fatherhood—you can just turn back around and step up. Both offer second chances.

There's an award given in SEAL training that's called First Time, Every Time. It's given to guys who went all the way through training without failing anything. (There's also an award called Fire in the Gut that usually goes to the guy who had the toughest time but made it through anyway.) Because of the dynamic and random nature of SEAL training, very few guys earn this award. However, at graduation, they receive no special recognition for never having failed a single evolution. *Nothing.* They get the same graduation certificate as the rest of us.

We all trip on our own dicks from time to time. It's not about perfection. It's about learning from our mistakes and picking ourselves up when we fall down. Never quitting is about always trying again. And this book isn't about a group of guys who flawlessly executed fatherhood. (I've found the books that contain only flawless execution to be bullshit.) It's about the dudes who had their share of failures and are sharing the best of what they got.

Captain Smith covered a lot of ground in a short amount of time, but one thing that has always stuck with me was his explanation about how each facet of our training was designed not just to build us as individuals but to assess and build our ability to function as

n. Over the years, I've come to think of SEAL operations arenting as evolving in a similar way, as a series of progres- phases that continuously increase in both complexity and consequence. The demands of fatherhood change over the course of our children's lives, from the very basic to the very complex, and a family's ability to weather those changes comes in large part through its capacity to work as a unit. In the end, the ability of SEALs and parents to dominate is determined by our collective training, communication, and overall desire to achieve. Teamwork!

FIRST PHASE
SEAL TRAINING: Week 1 to Week 7
PARENTING: Newborn to Age 2

First Phase of SEAL training is called Basic Conditioning Phase, which is like telling a fighter you're going to *basically condition* him to take a punch by repeatedly hitting him in the face with a hammer. It's a bit of a cruel and deceiving understatement. The object is to train a SEAL candidate in an environment where his mistakes and failures can do little harm to others. It's designed to bring men to their true limits and identify and eliminate those incapable of making the journey—or unwilling to make it.

First Phase takes place at the Center—a small compound that's protected by fences, surveillance cameras, armed guards, and the SEALs who run the training. It's not much to look at; the only thing that is striking about it is that there is nothing striking about it.

Anchoring the Center is a two-story, dirty-looking beige stucco building that stands alongside old military cinder-block offices, creating the feel of a prison yard without the bars. In the center of the buildings is what looks like a large courtyard but in SEAL parlance is known as the Grinder, named for its rough-painted texture, which has the propensity to sand the skin right off your ass as you do thousands of sit-ups. If there weren't a hundred SEAL trainees working out on it, you'd only know it by the small swim fins painted on the ground to indicate where students are supposed to line up for physical training (PT).

In front of the Grinder is a small blue wooden platform, which is where the instructors lead PT, and all around the platform is a breezeway held up by metal poles that have metal crossbars welded to them for doing pull-ups. Beyond the compound are old three-story barracks, where trainees stay during First Phase, and a parking lot, which leads to the beach. There you'll find another small blue wooden platform, from which instructors lead beach PT, and a tower with several large ropes you'll climb up and down until your hands, the best I could tell, start to bleed. Just past the ropes is a steep sand berm and then finally the cold Pacific Ocean. SEAL training is really quite basic and primitive—pull-up bars, sand, cold water, rope. There's not much to it. It flies in the face of modern and overly technical fitness methodologies. Here, you just do the work, and the work works.

During First Phase, SEAL students are constantly tested—physically and mentally. They must withstand extreme duress under pressure and observation in order to make sure that they, as individuals, are fit—and a *good fit*—for the team. The instructors endlessly push the students while watching their personal and group ethics to make sure that each man is stable, reliable, and able to maintain attention to detail whether sleep-, body-temp-, or energy-deprived. The belief is that only in this pressure cooker of physical and mental assault can a man's true will—what he's really committed to—be observed.

Throughout First Phase, SEAL trainees undergo continuous physical evolutions. You run obstacle courses while dry, and you run obstacle courses while wet. You paddle small boats through waves that slam you onto the sand, and you paddle small boats through waves that slam you onto the rocks. In the water, out of the water, again and again and again. In a day, you do thousands of flutter kicks that result in making the act of lifting your legs temporarily impossible. You do push-ups on the cement, on the sand, and in the water. You do sit-ups with giant logs on your chest and pull-ups until the skin is ripped from your hands. In the water, out of the water, again and again and again. You run hundreds of miles without rubber boats grinding the skin off your head and hundreds more *with* rubber boats grinding the skin off your head. I can remember swimming for so long in the cold, open ocean that—and I'm being serious here—my balls quit on me and tucked themselves into the warm safety of my pelvis. (The crazy thing is that I was so committed to what I was doing that I just kept going, accepting the fact that they might be gone for good!) All of these physical evolutions occur under the close watch of the instructor staff. They are always working to identify any sliver of mental instability or weakness. Their aim is not to evaluate SEAL candidates when they're at their best but to evaluate them at their worst. Nobody gives a damn how you act when you're winning.

Trainees repetitively cycle through these evolutions until muscle failure, until they absolutely can't do them anymore. And then it starts all over again—all day long. It's very much a 9-to-5 hammering like in that old cartoon where the sheepdog checks in, beats up the coyote, and then checks out after a full day's work. The instructors want you to recover overnight so that they can hit you again the next day. That's what makes SEAL training so difficult, the constant push/rest—the instructors bring you to your brink, and then they let you recuperate so that they can push you again and again. The instructors want you to know how to mend yourself when you get injured, and to do that, they give you the chance to let your body rest so you can rebuild, like a rubber band. If you stretch a rubber band farther than it can go, it will break and be done. The painful ordeal ends quickly. However, if you pull the rubber band only as far as it will allow, then rest, and then pull it again, then rest, you can stretch it farther and farther each time without breaking it. That's a whole lot of what they do in BUD/S.

SUGAR COOKIES

Sugar cookie has a unique meaning for SEALs. In BUD/S, if an instructor says, "Sugar cookie," that's an order for you to hit the cold surf and roll around in the wet sand until every inch of your body is covered. As a result, any PT exercise—running, going through an obstacle course, or simply standing still—can feel like torture as the salt and grains of sand itch, burn, and wear down your skin. It's like they took the notion of a beautiful, sweet sugar cookie and turned it into a sick and twisted method of pain and despair. Sugar cookie, my wet, sandy, and chafed ass!

Like SEAL training's First Phase, the beginning stage of parenting can be the most physically demanding. New parents lose countless hours of sleep (by the time we had our fourth kid, I would pretend I was sleeping so Belisa would get up) and endure nonstop physical evolutions as they chase those little bastards up and down every hallway, sidewalk, and mall. Instead of getting wet and sandy, they're getting puked and shat upon. Every trip out of the house is a perpetually changing obstacle course that is sometimes done wet, and other times done wet. And then you throw in crying babies, walking down the hallway for the fifth time in the middle of the night hoping you don't trip on the baby gate and fall down the stairs (or hoping that you do), spiked fevers you can't seem to break—the constant doubt of not knowing what to do or when it will end.

The First Phase of parenting is about having no control. It's not a time to ask why but to do or die. Although you signed up for this shit and are totally committed, the circumstances feel beyond you. Bottom line: You're getting your ass handed to you on a regular basis. You're in survival mode. You think to yourself, *If I can only make it through this next evolution, I'll be okay.* And then you think the same thing again during the next evolution and the next until somehow, against all odds, your commitment takes you through to the other side, gaining a little confidence each day, and you find yourself in the next phase, which will bring with it its own set of challenges and opportunities but also its own rewards. If I were to give advice to someone going into SEAL training, it would be the same thing I'd say to someone having a kid: Maintain your composure, don't get hurt, and never quit.

SECOND PHASE
SEAL TRAINING: Week 8 to Week 14
PARENTING: Age 2 to Age 17

During Second Phase, or Combat Diving Phase, SEAL candidates train to become combat swimmers with a curriculum that includes open- and closed-circuit diving as well as classes in dive physics, dive medicine, and dive rescue. As training progresses, so

HELL WEEK

Hell Week takes place during the fourth week of First Phase. It's everything you've heard about and more—kind of like the first week of parenting. From Sunday through Friday, SEAL candidates are either in painful motion or suffering in cold, muscle-cramping stillness. Every eight hours, a fresh crew of SEAL instructors descends upon the class with their bullhorns and their creative ways to get you to quit—they tell you that they've already decided that you aren't good enough or that all of the instructors want to get rid of you, or they'll set up tables with warm coffee and doughnuts and offer you one if you'll just give up. Students run over 200 miles and sleep less than four hours over the course of a whole week. It's a blur of pain and agony. Flashbacks of wild hallucinations of sharks and miniature men, as well as faint memories of sleeping while running with a boat on my head, lovingly haunt me to this day.

do the complexity and consequences for each member of the team, making teamwork all the more critical.

In this phase, one mistake can now cost more than one's personal failure or injury—it can get another person killed. The diving you do is so dark and so dangerous that you must be tethered to your *dive buddy,* a fellow SEAL candidate whom you have chosen or who has been assigned to you, at all times. It's a *Where you go, I go* situation, even if that means you're going to the bottom of the ocean permanently. No longer is training simply about being tough and not quitting. It's about learning, planning, and executing technical skills with another person in order to safely and successfully complete a mission. Fail to properly plan a dive, and the results can at a minimum get you both dropped from training, and at worst get you both killed.

During the first part of Second Phase, students are kept in an environment in which they can only harm themselves until they pass what is called Pool Comp, which can best be described as underwater attempted murder. Pool Comp begins with each candidate sitting with his back facing an Olympic-sized swimming pool, with a pair of black twin-80 SCUBA tanks strapped to his back, a black dive mask wrapped around his wrist, dive booties on his feet, and a set of black fins by his side.

My usual advice, when it comes to the testing process during SEAL training, is *not* to go first. However, during Pool Comp, trust me, you want to go first. I remember sitting there with my back to the pool, not being allowed to turn around and see what was happening. I could only hear what was going on, and what was going on didn't sound good: the sounds of free-flowing pressurized air bursting from SCUBA hoses and garbling as it reentered the water; thrashing-water noises that were drowned out only by the pleading of *Please stop!* and *I can't breathe!,* followed by the calm voices of the instructors saying, "We need a medic" or "You failed, failed, failed. Out of the pool. You suck."

Think punches to the gut, masks ripped off, and air hoses tied into knots tight enough to scare the hell out of Houdini. Every exercise is designed to test your ability to ignore your desire to both breathe and live, and to demonstrate your ability to follow procedure even if it feels like it's at your own peril. This is your first chance to demonstrate that you're worthy to be physically attached to another SEAL candidate, while diving on pure oxygen underneath large navy destroyers in order to plant simulated explosives in the black of night.

Once you pass Pool Comp, you are ready to learn to dive using a LAR V, a German-built closed-circuit rebreather system in which the diver's exhaled air is recirculated within the system rather than discharged as target-indicating bubbles into the surrounding enemy water. Basically, there's a small bottle of oxygen that feeds a—no kidding—bag from which you breathe. Your exhaled air goes through a scrubbing agent that looks like cat litter. This scrubber removes the carbon dioxide from your exhaled air and recycles your unused oxygen, resulting in no air bubbles in the water and no significant sound. These dives can last up to four hours and are particularly dangerous because oxygen at high levels (like those that are produced by breathing while under the compression of deep water) can poison your body and kill you. Same goes for the scrubbing agent used to remove the carbon dioxide—if it gets saltwater in it, it will turn into what's called a *caustic cocktail,* which can burn your throat and the inside of your lungs.

Since these dives are conducted in pure darkness, you are tethered to your dive buddy so that you don't lose him. That is why it is so important to know that the person you're attached to will calmly follow procedure, even if he thinks he's dying, because if he panics and shoots toward the surface, both of you can fail and/or be killed. During Dive Phase you've been determined worthy of having someone else's fate in your hands and tied to your own. You've been made a part of a team, and the team's actions must transcend the immediate situation and individual concerns in favor of collective and lasting consequences.

100 PERCENT PERSONAL ACCOUNTABILITY

Navy SEALs aren't robots. They're not immune to resentment. If a dive buddy's not stepping up to what's expected of him, leaving you to do all the work, fuck yeah, we're pissed off. Fights happen. Even so, we pull his ass through the swim, because that's what we need to do to get the job done. There is zero room for anything less than 100 percent personal accountability.

"Navy SEALs are the best of the best at what they do. People do not understand how loyal and close they are to one another and how willing they are to die to keep each other alive. I also see these guys as family—they were the guys at my birthday parties when I was a kid and at our family barbecues."

—JASON DAVIS

Dive teams work in tandem not just for safety but for effect. For instance, during underwater navigation, SEALs use a TAC board, a small plastic blackboard featuring a compass and a timer. If you're on the TAC board and leading the dive, you can't see—you're working the equipment—so you're essentially flying blind and depending on the other guy, like a copilot, to observe you; he monitors your O_2 toxicity, watches out for dangerous sea life, and makes sure that as fatigue sets in you don't lose sight of important details, such as diving too deep, which can kill you both. Additionally, each member of this small team must be able to back up, support, and hold each role; he must be able to pivot between responsibilities.

That's why SEALs dominate the battlefield—we support, guide, and fill in for one another seamlessly when needed.

As with SEAL training, the Second Phase of parenting is no longer about individual survival or endurance or merely staying awake. It is during this stage that you develop the technical knowledge and know-how beyond diapers and caffeine, and collaborate with your partner to teach your children how to work with and relate to others to accomplish their mission. Language and the gathering of knowledge are crucial components at this stage, as children absorb information and learn that their words and the words of others, particularly yours, guide, shape, and determine behavior and their ability to hit their targets or accomplish their missions. As in Dive Phase, it is our ability—ours and our children's—to take on and utilize technical and fundamental knowledge that determines success or failure. The habits and experiences formed here can, and often do, last a lifetime. When your children go into life's Pool Comp, they will be relying on what they learned during this time with you. When they enter the water, they can do nothing but fall back on their training.

During Second Phase, the *team* that you've become begins to take shape as individual roles and responsibilities become more defined and critical to success. Just as parents are tethered to one another—they are essentially dive buddies, *Where you go, I go*— our children learn how to depend on others, whom they can depend on, and how others can depend on them. They start learning how to find and develop their own dive buddies, making it critical that we, as parents, take on that SEAL instructor role to ensure the buddies they're tethering themselves to will not cause them failure or harm. Raising kids is more than just scheduling playdates with friends.

It's essential that during this time you become technically proficient as a team and that each team member is able to observe, monitor, and pivot between roles. Again, this isn't much different from the SEAL dive pairs: One (traditionally, but not necessarily, the father) will focus on navigating to the distant objective, while the other (spouse or significant other) will keep the team healthy, safe, and operational by maintaining the team's ability to "plan their dive and dive their plan." Whether you are married, single, or divorced, you must operate as a united front. Remember, if one parent, or dive buddy, bolts to the surface or takes a dive to the bottom, he or she can kill the rest of the team. Therefore, you have to count on each other, watch out for each other, and be able to step in and take over for each other when needed. You must follow procedure and rely on your training, even if it feels like it's at your own peril. Like SEAL training, parenting is now, and forever will be, *we* before *me.* Act accordingly.

MY DIVE BUDDY QUIT. NOW WHAT?

As life sometimes goes, dive buddies can become separated, either by choice or by circumstance. I got divorced after I already had two kids. However, Stacey, my ex-wife, and I were committed to our children and realized that what was best for them was for us to remain "tethered" as parents—we remained a single united front of love and discipline.

Both Stacey and I eventually remarried, and Belisa, my wife, and Scott, Stacey's husband, had the same attitude: We wanted to stay tight as a team (Scott and I have actually coached the kids' soccer teams together) and do the best by the kids. Of course, it was a challenge, and there is no doubt that every member of the team had to frequently—and without complaint—acquiesce or swallow chunks of pride in order to remain unified. To this day, the four of us "co-parent" as a team, because we're not selfishly focused on ourselves or putting our own desire for personal comfort or preference before the needs of the team.

I know that our relationship is uncommon, but that shouldn't be the case. If you've found your way into a single-parent situation by way of a divorce or a split-up—pay attention, dads, because we're usually the ones to fuck this part up—it's on *you* to make the relationship work well enough so that you can continue to parent together. That means the same rules and way of life in both houses. None of this *you can have candy for dinner* bullshit. That also means that if you married a crazy bitch, it's on you to suck it up and deal with it, because she's *your* crazy bitch and for you to love as the mother of your children.

THIRD PHASE
SEAL TRAINING: Week 15 to Week 21
PARENTING: Age 14 to Age 18

In the Third Phase of BUD/S, Land Warfare, SEAL candidates learn basic weaponry and small-unit tactics. Essentially, they learn how to effectively deploy assault rifles, grenades, C-4 plastic explosives, TNT, and the tub-shaped Bangalore torpedoes used by our Underwater Demolition Team (UDT) forefathers from World War II.

Throughout SEAL training, instructors have been carefully monitoring both the performance and attitudes of each SEAL candidate, so that by the time he gets to Third Phase, they can be certain that he will not kill the entire class. They want to hammer in cause and consequences while dealing with high-powered weapons. Safety violations occur when SEAL trainees fail to follow a procedure—such as how to safely break down and rebuild an M-60 machine gun, or how to set up an electric blasting range—to perfection. Think of it as an all-out final assault on the SEAL student. This is the last chance the instructors have to get rid of someone who doesn't belong in the community. The instructors know that either they or one of their teammates will potentially be going to war with one of these guys, and once a guy makes it all the way through SEAL training, there is nothing the instructors can do to him. Therefore, SEAL training is as much about protecting the community as it is about preparing a candidate to enter it. We're basically creating high-functioning citizens who will both excel within and improve the community they enter. (Imagine the world in which we would live if all parents did and thought the same for themselves and their kids.)

The need to pay attention to detail cannot be overstated, and the penalties for not doing so are a cruel and unusual reminder of how very seriously the instructors take this portion of the training. Because candidates have already gone through such adversity and have built up a sufficient amount of confidence as they close in on graduation, any documented instance that states their demonstrated incompetence becomes a harsh (but manageable) hit to their ego. And that's just what the instructors want to do—hit their ego to carve away any arrogance that may still reside there. It's a forging process that requires some heat.

Or, in this case, ice.

Enter the Slushy—an entirely new form of penalty in which

the instructors load ice into a large vat (which, ironically, is normally used to cook warm soup for hundreds of people) and add cold water, bringing the temperature down so far that it can only be calculated on the scale that measures the degree to which your human soul is sucked out of you. (To totally understand this, I need you to go to your kitchen and fill a large bowl to the top with ice, add cold water, and stick your hand in it for sixty seconds. Now, imagine doing that to your entire body—repetitively.) Every mistake in Third Phase has the potential to cause death or dismemberment, and the Slushy serves as a stand-in for or reminder of the ultimate consequence for even the most minor error. The Slushy was the only thing I truly feared in BUD/S.

Since SEALs are constantly armed with and deploying high-powered weapons as part of their craft, it is imperative—not only to their safety but to the safety of anyone within a 5-mile radius—that they're able to respect, manage, and control every aspect of every weapon they use. By experiencing cause and consequence in an unaltered and unsoftened environment, SEALs are able to develop their sense of personal responsibility and the autonomies required to succeed. They are trained to be responsible for every outcome, because they are free to control it. They are never victims of circumstance, always masters of their own universe.

Similarly, as our sons age, the complexity of their choices increases along with their accountability and their freedom to make those choices, creating potential consequences that can significantly impact the entire team. Your goal as a parent is to build a team of strength and confidence, and to provide your son a solid foundation before heavy correction is necessary or applied. You are handing over the reins, but still watching and correcting until you believe he is ready to make choices on his own.

As my first two children, Taylor and Jason, got older, Stacey and I backed off a little too much. As a result, we noticed the kids starting to produce some minor safety violations (credit card debt, dropping out of college, getting too tied up in relationships) that, if left unchecked, could turn into major ones. Jason would say things like "I think someone should hire me just because I'm Jason," which sounds kind of cute and funny right up until the moment you realize that he might actually believe it. Then it just sounds fucking stupid and dangerous. Stacey and I realized that with the reins off it wasn't time to sit back but time for an all-out assault of parenting. It was time to step back in and give them the verbal Slushies that they needed—and, deep down, desired.

> *"Eric was the only one in his platoon who had kids when we first met. It was strange to see someone who was a SEAL but also a parent, because in my mind they didn't go together. Eric's parenting style, and now our parenting style, has always been different from other couples' and from what I always thought my parenting style would be. I believe that does come from the Teams. I swear they reprogram their brains when they are in training, so they don't see, think, speak, or live like normal people. Our kids started swimming when they were months old, they were rock climbing once they knew how to grab onto a hold, and they were placed in backpacks and taken everywhere—mountains, beach, desert, no place was off-limits. None of the kids can keep up with him—even to this day—but they all try."*
>
> **—BELISA DAVIS**

TRAINING NEVER ENDS

Most people assume that upon completion of BUD/S that SEAL training is over, but this is no truer than assuming that parenting is over once a child turns eighteen. The skill sets learned in each of the three phases of BUD/S are expanded upon in SEAL Qualification Training (SQT), an abbreviated version of a SEAL platoon workup. Qualified SEAL platoons spend eighteen months training and rehearsing for deployment; sending someone into a SEAL platoon after just six months of training would be like asking him to catch up with a jet. SQT gets people up to speed so that they can integrate with an experienced platoon.

Upon successful completion of SQT, candidates become qualified SEALs. They join the SEAL Teams and get their Special Warfare insignia, the Navy SEAL Trident—a large gold emblem that consists of an eagle holding a navy anchor, a trident, and a flintlock-style pistol. For the SEAL, the eagle represents his ability to vanquish his enemies from the air and a reminder that the SEALs' standards should soar above any other force's. (If you look closely, you'll notice that, in ornamentation, most eagles are portrayed with their head held high. The eagle on a SEAL Trident has his head lowered to remind warriors to remain humble and strong.) Throughout their careers, Navy SEALs will continue their formal education with all kinds of advanced training— military freefall, sniper school, advanced demolitions, intelligence training, and much more.

Similarly, when our sons turn eighteen, it's not time to "let go" and stop being a father. Up until that point, we have provided many *guardrails*—constant supervision aimed at producing an environment where trainees, or children, can make the right decisions and build up strength, confidence, and responsibility. Once they reach adulthood, this is the time for some of the most critical and complex parenting that we'll do, since they've begun to settle into their ways and, of course, know it all. This is our last shot at refining their training to ensure that they enter into the world and not only flourish within it but, more importantly, improve it. Here, more than any other time in their lives, I've had to be my children's father, not their friend.

Those early phases of SEAL training, as with parenting, merely set the stage and build the foundation for lifelong instruction and practice. Beyond that, SEAL students, and our children, enter what I like to call the Fourth Phase of training, the one that has no time limit and never ends. If the mission is to create capable, kind, and civilly minded kids, the only way to accomplish that is through lifelong teamwork, collective intelligence, and coordinated action. As Captain Smith explained in class that day in First Phase, when it comes to a high-functioning team, there's no room for a Rambo.

DAVID RUTHERFORD: THE POWER OF COMMUNICATION

David Rutherford is a top motivational speaker, behavioral training specialist, author for kids and adults, and performance coach. He served eight years in the Naval Special Warfare Community as a SEAL student, combat paramedic, operator, and instructor. After his honorable discharge from the navy in 2003, he continued honing his skills as a tactical training and security expert for the U.S. government and one of the largest private security firms in the world until he finally hung up his bulletproof vest in fall 2011. In 2006, he founded Froglogic Concepts, a motivational entertainment company whose primary mission is to provide Navy SEAL motivational training for civilians, young and old, through a perpetual stream of high-quality, inspiring, and positive free content. He derives his Froglogic philosophy from his twenty-five years of exploring and researching the human condition, combined with seventy-plus years of UDT/Navy SEAL operations, training doctrine, and elite performance. David's new mission in life is to help corporate teams, organizations, schools, nonprofits, and individuals learn how to embrace their fear, forge their self-confidence, and live the Team Life with purpose. Since starting Froglogic, Rutherford has reached over four million people worldwide, including more than fourteen thousand schoolchildren across North America, with his message. He has two daughters, ages five and three.

Lack of communication is really a significant problem with most companies around the country right now, especially within HR departments. In the world of the Navy SEALs, if you have an issue with someone, you go straight to him. You're going to bring whatever it is to his attention and deal with it right there. If he can't deal with it, you go to the next person in your chain of command. Nine times out of ten, that conflict will never work its way outside of the platoon, or the immediate little group in which you operate. Out in the real world, man, people jump the chain of command all the time, like it's not even an issue. They don't even recognize the challenge it places on the hierarchal structure of a normal organization and on the people who have assigned responsibilities. They just jump command, and if they don't get what they want, they either quit or file a grievance or threaten a lawsuit.

I try to help companies create and work better recruiting systems, and one of the scariest statistics out there is this: By the time the average young person is thirty-three to thirty-five years old, he has had seven different careers—not seven different jobs within the same industry but seven different *careers*. That's an *astronomical* number. *Oh, if this doesn't feel good, I'm going to try something else.* This statistic tells me two things about the frivolous nature of how people go to work:

1. So many of our young people have never been forced to really take a good look at what they want to do in their life.
2. They don't know how to deal with adversity. When something goes wrong or gets really hard in their career, rather than tackling it head-on, they just quit.

Just in my little company alone, I've lost three young people in the last six months, and it was because of the challenge of the work, the amount of work, the speed of the work, and the demands required when working for a SEAL. I think it was too much for them. They weren't used to it.

Everything we are ultimately boils down to the influences we've had in our life, and so many parents are shucking off their responsibilities to actually *influence* their children. How often do you hear people say *I don't want to pressure my kid* or *I want to let him come to his own decision?* They think they're helping their child, but if they don't foster any sense of drive, where do they expect the drive to come from?

I recently asked my five-year-old daughter, "What do you want to be when you grow up?" I ask her this all the time, and the answer changes, but right now she wants to be a bunny farmer. I immediately said, "Yeah, that'd be a great idea. You could be the top-selling bunny farmer in the world. You could sell their pelts, you could sell their meat, you could sell . . ." Meanwhile, she's looking at me cross-eyed, but that doesn't matter. I chat with her about the realistic nature of drive and competition and accountability. That's what matters.

DEBRIEF

+ What does quitting being a father look like to you? What are some examples of quitting you've seen in others and yourself?

+ Do the dive buddies your kids choose help them with their mission or hurt them? Do they produce confidence in your children? Is this something you monitor daily?

+ What are the roles and responsibilities of each member of your team?

+ How do you and the members of your team pivot between roles and support one another?

2

LEAD FROM THE FRONT

I was sitting in Dulles International Airport in Washington, D.C., after having spent weeks in special preparation for a top-secret mission on the opposite side of the planet. Once a week, the CIA would have a plane pick us up and take us into a country where no American was allowed. It would be our job to develop relationships and smuggle in equipment and weapons so that the U.S. forces, and/or the forces that came behind us, could take up arms, move around, or escape.

For this particular mission, I had learned the finer points of staying alive if captured by terrorists, how to avoid spending the rest of my life being tortured in an enemy's prison, and sophisticated surveillance skills and methods of surreptitious entry that would allow my three-man SEAL element to gain access to just about anything that we wanted to. I had been briefed by every major intelligence agency I had ever heard of, and some I hadn't heard of, and was on my way to carry out their wishes.

To go on missions like this meant that you were an Advanced Force Operations (AFO) operative, one who conducts clandestine operations in areas typically not occupied by or permissive to U.S. forces or allies. AFO teams go out ahead of all other forces to conduct operational preparation of the battlespace. To be on one of them required a special selection process and, for me, represented the pinnacle of being a SEAL.

As I sat in the airport that day, wrestling with the guilt from leaving home once again, I realized that a large part of being a father is going out—alone—to prepare the environment. It's often part of our role to leave the family behind to recon and plan the routes to life's meaningful objectives—health, happiness, purpose, helping others. Particularly in today's knowledge-fueled and technologically advanced world, fathers must always keep multiple steps ahead of their families to reinforce the right path, to scout out the next step, and to make sure the battlefield has been surveyed and prepared in order to come back and lead our families through it. Then it's out again and back to lead.

> "Being asked about my father is a very difficult question, because there is an inside and an outside—outside being that he is a super-cool elite warrior who's jumping out of planes in the middle of the night, and inside being his never-ending effort to make sure he spends time with us as a dad and makes us happy. I know, at times, he will feel guilty if he thinks he is working too long and therefore losing time with us. However, we understand. Everyone has to work, and the time not with us is when he is working to support all of us."
>
> **—JASON DAVIS**

> *"Over the years, we have come to realize that we can lead our kids, but they have to be the ones to choose what path they want to follow. All we can do is be the people we want our kids to be and lead by example. A lot of what Eric learned in the SEAL Teams was from the instructors leading by example. The instructors can do every evolution on the O Course; they completed freefall school and SQT. They achieved success in more ways than just monetary rewards. They earned their Trident and are now showing the others how to earn theirs. That is how Eric parents, by leading. It is all he has ever known."*
>
> —BELISA DAVIS

LIKE FATHER, LIKE SON

As a kid, I always knew what kind of man I wanted to be. I wanted to be like my father, a person others would look up to and count on when things were at their worst. Having served in our nation's military as a marine, he was also the bishop of our church and a captain in the San Mateo County's Sheriff's Department. My father stood at a commanding six foot three with black hair and olive skin, and by the age of seventeen, I had but one purpose in life—to prepare myself to become a sheriff. Just like him. Although I wasn't old enough to enter law enforcement training, I was anxious to start preparing, and that led me to the military.

In 1990, I visited the Army Recruiting Office, where I learned about the legendary Army Rangers and that I could be a medic with them. Instantly, I signed up in the army's Delayed Entry Program, since I was only seventeen, thinking that the medical knowledge would make me an even better sheriff. As I learned more about the various military options there were, I became hooked; the amount of training and possibilities seemed endless.

Soon after I enlisted, the movie *Navy SEALs* came out—yes, the one with Charlie Sheen—and I learned that there was a Special Forces unit that focused on the ocean. Being a surfer, I thought that would be the way to go. I went into the Navy Recruiting Office, and the recruiters showed my best friend, Jay, and me a video about being a SEAL. It looked so gnarly that Jay said, "That looks too crazy." That was it. The moment I realized that being a SEAL was the most difficult thing I could do, I knew it was what I *had* to do. We went to the Army Recruiting Office and got let out of our contracts so we could enlist in the navy. (Jay never ended up going to SEAL training. After several years, he got out of the navy and went into the army, where he is thriving as a warrant officer. Leadership was always in his blood.)

Eventually, my ambition grew to a deep, unwavering desire to become three things—a Navy SEAL, a sniper, and a point man. I may have been too young and inexperienced at the time to realize it, but the primary purpose of all of these roles was to prepare and train to a high degree, so that I could go out ahead and lead—just like my dad—and prepare the way for others to accomplish their missions. People would need me to get to where they wanted to go.

When we think of snipers we tend to focus on their ability to engage and eliminate targets from a great distance, which, while important, is not their primary purpose. Before any mission is conducted, shot is taken, or target is assaulted, *someone* has been there first. A sniper is that someone. He has trained relentlessly to master skills such as camouflage, concealment, and movement, and he has used those skills to access the seemingly impossible areas from which he can observe and report on the enemy. Snipers do the reconnaissance work necessary to figure out how to exploit and dominate their areas of operation. It is only once they have done those things that they serve as an overwatch, guiding and protecting their team as it penetrates in order to take the target.

While being a sniper is not a prerequisite to becoming a point man, it is definitely helpful, because the roles are similar. A point man is the member of a SEAL platoon who walks, climbs, or crawls ahead of the rest. His job is to plan the routes to and from a target, then lead the platoon there. As a point man, it is your primary duty to break new ground—sometimes in the wrong direction—and see what lies ahead, so that you can bring the other members of the team safely past any threats and to their objective, and remain with them to help accomplish the mission.

Walking point—being the first man on patrol, literally the "point" of the spear—requires levels of alertness that, once developed, never go away. Since SEALs primarily operate in harsh and unfamiliar territories, the point man is arguably one of the most exposed positions and is considered very dangerous, because it's highly likely that whatever threat he comes upon he'll momentarily face alone, before his platoon is able to get to him.

Similarly, being the point man of your family team means that sometimes you will have to go out ahead and take time away from them. You're going to have to *leave*—not to become an absentee father but to be the knowledgeable and relevant father your son needs. If you're not leading from the front, being the person you want your children to be, then you will not be able to show them the way. You need to *be* as well as *be there* or else the whole thing backfires.

I find that men have difficulty with that. Trust me, I get it. As a SEAL father, I used to struggle with leaving my kids behind for what could sometimes be nine months out of a year. I couldn't participate in Boy Scouts or stuff like that. It sucked to be gone, but sometimes that's what it takes.

In the world of human intelligence, there's a concept called *placement and access.* This means that in order to obtain the battle plans of another country, you need an agent who is already working in the place that contains the plans and has access to the plans themselves. Our sons need the battle plans for a good life, and it is up to us to *place* ourselves in such a way that we can *access* the strategies and tactics required to live it. They need us to be their agents in the field. We must infiltrate success. You can physically be next to your son twenty-four hours a day, but if you are not experiencing a good life and teaching him to do the same, then you may as well be gone. Conversely, you can be away from your son for months at a time, but if you're living a life of example and he

BRO TIME

Many fathers, in a valiant though misguided effort to support their family, will sacrifice bro time—time spent being active with the fellas. This can impact their health and happiness and will eventually take them out of the game. When left uncared for, we can turn to drugs and alcohol or other unhealthy habits in an effort to fill this need for activity. This is a lesson I know and have taught to those around me the hard way, because I'm a miserable son of a bitch if I'm not active enough. Men were bred to hunt and fight, and in modern environments where that is no longer required, we use sports and adventure to fulfill that need (we'll discuss this in more depth in chapter 9). For the bulk of our existence on this planet, we were out with the boys hunting while trying not to get hunted. Dumping beer down our throats and watching TV ain't gonna get it done.

can access it—via phone, e-mail, or video chat with you—then this all can work. ₁

There are very few dudes out there just crushing life and being the person that they want their son to be. Too many (at times, myself included) hamster into their home lives, because they are either feeling too guilty about doing what they need to do or, worse, using "family time" as an excuse not to get out there, get healthy, and kill it in their careers. Being home is valuable and important when it comes to raising our sons; however, it's not the objective. *Where* you are doesn't trump *who* you are, because sometimes—despite your best intentions—you may not be around when your son needs you most. ₁

MAN DOWN

One morning, shortly before my sixteenth birthday, I came down the stairs of our townhouse to find my mother and father standing in our dining room as if waiting for me to enter. My mother explained that my father was sick and needed to go to the hospital. When I looked at my dad, he broke into tears.

"I don't feel good," he choked out. Unbeknownst to me, he had been struggling with depression for many years. "I have to go away to get better."

After that day, everything changed. My dad would no longer have a consistent physical presence in my life. We stopped going to church. We stopped spending regular time together. (My mother, who had been a bishop's wife for many years, wound up leaving her religion and the lifestyle that came with it. At age seventy-five, she swears like a trucker and is a bit different than she was when I was a kid, but her love and support for me have never faltered.)

At fifteen years old, I was too young to be without my father but old enough to know I still needed him, which propelled me on a lifelong pursuit of self-exploration that included the relentless studying of psychology, performance, and every bit of self-help discourse I could find. I was in desperate search of a mentor. With my dad gone, I lost not only my role model but a bit of my own identity. It was like having the string to my kite cut. I began to drift.

Rather than having purpose and direction, my life was going nowhere. The summer after my father became ill, I took off with my buddies on a surfing/camping trip to San Onofre State Beach in San Clemente, California, in an old, beat-up Chevy van that had surf stickers all over it and huge speakers that would literally shake the van apart when we turned up the bass. (The people camping next to us must have been horrified as, several times a day, we reenacted a scene out of *Fast Times at Ridgemont High* and rolled out of the smoke-filled van.) On the final night of our trip, we stopped by my grandmother's house in Seal Beach, which was only thirty minutes north on the I-5 freeway, and it would be a decision that would change my life.

"Tell me about Grandpa," I said to her that night. My grandfather, like my father, had been one of my favorite people. He died when I was nine or ten years old.

My grandmother began to share stories of my great-grandfather, who was a sheriff like my father, and of my grandfather's time in the navy and how he served under J. Edgar Hoover as a G-man (for "government man") in the FBI. I remember feeling grounded as she filled in some of the blanks in my family history. It was the reconnection I had been craving as my father's illness progressed and our ability to spend time together continued to fade. I realized our modified relationship could be a responsibility, not a liability. Though he's been sick and in a nursing home for almost half of my life, he's still been able to lead and guide me the entire time—not through constant counsel and time spent together but by having lived a life, as long as he could, that he wanted me to live. And it was that realization that led me to the Army and Navy Recruiting Offices and into a lifelong pursuit of service.

BLUE AND GOLD

A SEAL instructor's T-shirt is blue and gold. It has the words UDT/SEAL INSTRUCTOR in quarter-inch-high block letters written over the left side of the chest. UDT stands for Underwater Demolition Team, the father of today's Navy SEAL. When an instructor steps in front of a class of SEAL wannabes, he instantly has their respect and trust. This is how we want our kids to view us. We want them to see us as someone they want to emulate.

However, if it were only as easy as putting on a blue and gold shirt, I would not be writing this book. I would just pass out the T-shirts, and we'd be all good. Donning a SEAL instructor shirt was not what made me follow these guys. Rather, it was *who* was wearing the shirts that made me follow. It was what had been required of them to get that shirt that made me follow. These guys were *real,* and I really wanted to be like them.

EARNING THEIR TIME AND ATTENTION

The time with my father fostered a sense of respect and admiration in me that would last a lifetime, and I knew, as a parent, that

I needed to produce the same result with my own kids. When children are young, this is very easy to do—wiping your own ass or tying your shoes is pretty impressive to a three-year-old. The trick is holding and nurturing that respect with a thirteen-year-old who is spending more time with friends and has greater outside influences that will compete with yours.

When I spend time with my children, I make it a point to do extreme activities that I'm already very good at. This is because I want to create an environment in which two things occur:

+ I want them to feel uneasy, outside of their comfort zone, so that they'll have to look to me—and become used to looking to me—when things get heavy. My favorite place to build admiration, respect, and trust has always been in the water. I love the water, my children know my history as a SEAL and of all my accomplishments in the water, and there are few environments that are more daunting. It's not unheard of for me to give my kids a heavy kettle bell and make them do as many underwater laps as they can without passing out while only allowing them to take one single breath each time they surface, or to tie their hands and feet together as part of underwater drown-proofing training. In their early teens, I had Taylor and Jason race back and forth across the pool with weight belts strapped to their waists—again, only allowing a single breath per surfacing. Quickly, as they became physically stressed when their bodies began to crave air, they would fix their eyes on me. They knew that they could count on me to keep them safe as they stretched themselves further. (Remember that rubber band?)

"When we first started doing these drills, there was excitement in the this is what Dad does aspect, which would make me want to push myself harder. As the intensity of these drills picked up, which it did very quickly, I was comfortable with going past my limit line, because I knew that even before I started to go down, I would have been flung out of the pool by my dad. I know my dad was always worried about pushing too much of this stuff on us, but looking back, I wish we had stuck to these drills more over the years. I have not had one friend with even close to the amount of water confidence I have. There were times when friends of mine wouldn't go into the ocean because of the waves and I would jump into them, arms open. This ability has even allowed me to get people out of bad situations at the beach when huge sets of waves rolled in. I have been dragged deep to the bottom of the ocean hundreds of times and have never panicked. I remain calm, because I know my limits."

—JASON DAVIS

✦ I want to show off a bit and be one of the most interesting people in their life so that I will always have a place on their calendar. As a young parent, I'd spend countless hours in the water with my kids doing flips, dives, underwater piggyback rides, you name it. One day, while swimming at a barbecue, my daughter grabbed my ears, pulled my head close to hers so that we were eye to eye, and said, "Why aren't the other papas in the pool?" I looked around, and she was right. They weren't. They were sitting elsewhere, most likely tired from a long day or feeling lazy or overworked, or maybe they didn't like the water. Whatever the reason, my child noticed, and, I'll bet, *so did theirs.*

It's kind of funny—not ha-ha funny but weird funny—how many parents work hard to condition their kids to ignore them, or encourage the kids to go off and be with their friends. I watch many parents use playdates as a way to keep their children engaged and entertained, which inevitably makes anybody and everybody more interesting and useful than the parents are. Some parents go so far as to force their kids into unfruitful, or even harmful, relationships with other kids simply because they like hanging out with the parents of those kids. It's no wonder kids quickly lose interest in, and respect for, their parents. Parents have lost interest in, and respect for, them.

LIFELONG LEARNING

In order to lead, you must continue to learn. A big reason kids think they know it all and their parents are wrong is that kids are studying and growing every day and most parents have been out of the growth game since they left school. As time goes on, children begin to know more than their parents, and that infamous *I know everything* attitude begins to form in our teenage and adult sons. For example, if Dad no longer hunts, it'll only be a matter of time before his hunting son stops listening to him about how to hunt. The son views his father as trying to impart wisdom that he is no longer qualified to impart, and as he gets older he begins to intuit the hypocrisy, and respect is lost. It's okay that your kid thinks he knows more than you do. It's just not okay if he actually does.

LEAN ON ME

As a father, I always knew that it was important for my kids to depend on me, to lean on me for my power and support as they grew through life, but it wasn't until the Third Phase of SEAL training that I realized how much I depended on them for the same.

We were training at Mount Laguna, California, nearly 6,000 feet above sea level on the eastern edge of the Cleveland National Forest, immersing ourselves in the art and science of land navigation. We were only allowed to bring a minimal amount of gear and were not to be caught with anything extra, despite the fact that it was winter and there was snow. *A lot* of snow. After several days of hiking in bitterly cold temperatures and sleeping huddled up under a thin rain poncho, it was time to take our land navigation test.

I had already been through the Marine Basic Reconnaissance Course as a corpsman, and since I had learned land navigation well, I wasn't as worried as I should have been. About halfway through the test, I sat down in a shaded valley to change out the plastic bags that I had wrapped around my feet to keep out the wet snow. (Though SEALs have the best gear money can buy, SEAL trainees are relegated to common military issue.) As I pulled off the bags, I pulled off two of my toenails on my left foot as well. (I was actually quite fortunate, considering the situation. It was no big deal—I couldn't feel my toes anyway. To this day, I still can't feel them.)

The outside temperature quickly began to drop, and my body temperature was slowly doing the same. I began to shiver. Ahead of me was a ballbuster of a hill, so I got after it pretty hard, hoping I would warm up. On my way down the other side, my body shivered uncontrollably, and I felt the beautiful and hypnotic haze of exhaustion begin to set in. It wasn't until I reached the bottom that I realized I had gone over the wrong hill. *Fuck me.*

By this point, I was behind in time, dehydrated, and physically exhausted, but I pushed back over the hill as quickly as I could back down to where my bloody toenails lay. Weary and frozen, I gathered my composure and consulted my map and realized the good news: I hadn't gone the wrong way, after all. I had only read my map wrong. Wait, good news? I'd already gone over the right hill twice—there and back—and would now have to do it a third time. *Fuck me again!*

Fueled with anger, yet still dizzy from dehydration and hunger, I set out again, conquered the hill, and got back on track. Unfortunately, my mind and body weren't tracking with me, and both began to shut down; I was cold and confused and found myself stumbling back to camp yards at a time. Only six weeks away from graduation, the first real fears of not making it through training crept into my head. I started thinking about my next career. Law enforcement? Insurance sales? McDonald's? What would it be? I tried to stay positive. I knew there would be a retest the next day, which I was confident I would pass. It wasn't over yet.

> *"When I first got divorced, every time I'd visit the kids, I would take them shoe shopping. It took me a year to figure out why I was so obsessed with making sure my kids had the coolest shoes. I realized it was because when I was a kid, my dad would give my mom so much grief because I wanted a pair of Vans or Reeboks. All the other kids at school had them, and he refused to buy them for me. We'd go to*

the thrift store or the shitty shoe store, and I'd get whatever crap he would find, and it sucked. I remember my mom saving up to get me a pair of shoes, and I was so excited. I told my own kids the whole story, why I'm obsessed with their shoes, and we all had a laugh about it. Our experiences with our parents—good and bad—are what make us who we are, and it's important to be honest with kids about that, to share with them all the stuff that makes you you. Your leadership role should come from a place of honesty. When Gabriele and I decided to get a divorce and needed to tell the kids, we took them to a place that they really didn't care about, because we didn't want to ruin a park or a happy place by delivering the bad news, and we sat them down and were just honest. We all had a big hug and cried as a family, and it was incredibly tough (in some strange way it was beautiful), but I think the kids respected us for doing it that way, for our honesty, and our vulnerability with each other, which we've carried forward in our relationship ever since."

—BRANDON WEBB, FORMER NAVY SEAL

I collapsed when I got back to camp, delirious from dehydration and fatigue. As I removed my shirt in the cold snow, I heard my name being called by one of the SEAL instructors, who asked me what happened and whether I thought I could pass.

"*Hooyah,*" I said, which, at the moment, meant *I can do it.*

The instructor then informed me that the retest would be *that day,* not the next.

"*Hooyah,*" I said again, which this time meant *Oh, shit, I'm going to die.*

"Get your gear together," the instructor said. "You have one hour before you start."

I decided I'd better say something about my physical condition, since I knew from my time served as a medic that I was in trouble, but it came out as *Hooyah*. I kept saying the word over and over, as in *I think my body is going to shut down and go into hypothermia*. However, all the instructor heard was *Sure, I can retest now. I'll see you in an hour*.

Damn the *Hooyah*. Damn the *Hooyah* straight to hell.

Some of my fellow students saw that I was hurting and started what we so eloquently refer to as rat-fucking their MREs (Meals, Ready-to-Eat) to pull out the most energy-producing food they could find. I choked down as many M&M's and as much jalapeño cheese spread, cold spaghetti with meat sauce, and water as I could stomach. I had to recover fast if I was going to pass the retest—or at least survive it.

As I stepped out of camp, the fatigue returned almost instantaneously, and I felt the fear of not making it through training turn into real doubt: If I failed the retest, I was gone. In SEAL training, it's strike one, strike two—you're out!

I felt a tinge of panic. A thought came to me: Quitting the test might be the only way to survive it. However, at that very moment, another thought entered my mind: Taylor and Jason. I began to imagine what I'd do if they were there watching me. I imagined them standing on the side of the snow-covered trail. *Would you let them see you quit?* I asked myself.

No.

"*Hooyah*," I said silently to myself, this time meaning *I love you guys*. I remember this moment so well, because as I thought of Taylor and Jason I could feel the forest reset itself. It was as if it suddenly reshuffled and came back into focus.

I put my head down and went. A quarter of the way. Halfway. Three-quarters of the way. All I thought about was my map and my kids (and I occasionally wondered about my missing toenails). Things were getting so bad that another student, Joel McGuire, who was also a fellow corpsman, wouldn't let me out of his sight despite the fact that he himself could end up failing, or being accused of cheating, and be dropped from training.

Along the way, my body started to give out, and I fell to the ground. I had eaten every bit of food I had, and there was no more water. I thought of my kids watching me again.

"*Hooyah*," I said to myself, this time meaning *Fuck it*.

I got up.

Ten yards later, my legs gave out, not as in cramping or freezing up but as in just dropping out from under me.

"*Hooyah*." This one had no meaning. It just felt good to say it.

Medically speaking, it was too dangerous for me to continue, but I saw Joel shadowing me. *Hooyah*. I went down a few more times—once because my legs dropped out again and twice because I was trying to beat them to it.

As we got closer to camp, knowing that we couldn't arrive together, Joel looked at me and said, "I'm going to run in and let them know you're going down. Are you good?"

"*Hooyah*" slipped from my lips one final time. This one meant *I don't know*.

I remember Joel leaving and then bits and pieces of what happened next: a couple more falls, walking into camp, beginning to take off my clothes while standing in the snow. (Yes, it was as weird as it sounds.)

I woke up hours later with my good friend Chris Osman by my side. Chris is as tough as they come—a hardcore, tell-it-like-it-is, will-call-anyone-out-at-anytime kind of guy. When I came to, he looked as if he'd been crying.

ARE YOU WORTH LISTENING TO?

Kids are smart. They know when someone is bullshitting them. My middle school PE teacher must have been at least eighty pounds overweight, and he never let us play any games like soccer or baseball because it would require more work for him to set up. He'd always say, "PE is to get fit, not have fun." Instead of saying yes to our request to play sports, he would make us do boring exercises and try to teach fitness by rattling off facts about the body. We all knew it was because he was too lazy to organize the games for us, so I tuned him out. Why should I listen to *that guy*? What did he know about physical fitness? Then came high school and Mrs. Philpots. Wow, she was hot—and in shape. That lady could have told me to eat Twinkies for lunch and drink nacho cheese for dinner, and I would have done it. She *did* physical fitness. And I respected that.

"Goddamn it, dude," he said with emphasis. "I thought you were going to die!"

I always knew that being a father was an amazing responsibility, but it wasn't until SEAL training that I realized how much strength, power, and motivation I drew from it. It's easy to slip into the idea that the responsibility of being a father takes up a bunch of your time and holds you back, but that day, if it hadn't been for my children and knowing how they counted on me as their leader, their point man, I would have probably just lain there in the icy snow, letting time and my dreams—and myself—expire. I learned the value of respecting my children's respect. It was a lesson that saved my life.

CHRIS SAJNOG: FOOD FOR THOUGHT

Chris Sajnog is one of the most experienced and respected firearms trainers in the world, being hand-selected to develop the training for the U.S. Navy SEAL sniper program. As a Navy SEAL, he was the senior sniper instructor, a certified Master Training Specialist (BUD/S), and an advanced-training marksmanship instructor. After retiring from the SEAL Teams in 2009 to spend time with his family, Chris began training civilians and law enforcement officers. He is the founder of the New Rules of Marksmanship, a revolutionary approach to firearms training. Also a bestselling author, Chris has a passion for finding innovative ways to teach elite-level skills and now teaches thousands of students via online remote coaching. He lives in San Diego with his wife and two sons.

In 2008, when I had come home from my last deployment, my oldest son, who was four at the time, went through a period of almost two weeks in which he refused to eat his food. Everyone was trying to get him to eat, and he wouldn't.

One day I asked him, "Hey, buddy, why aren't you eating?"

Finally, he said, "If I eat, I'll grow up. If I grow up, I'll become a daddy, and if I become a daddy, I'll have to leave my family."

I grew up without a dad, and I wasn't going to do that to my boys. The next day, I put in my retirement papers, and that's the reason I left the SEAL Teams. I loved being a SEAL. I loved everything about it, and it was hard to give up being a part of that team, but in the end I have a commitment to my family and to my boys, making sure that I lead them properly. That was more important to me.

I was able to access something beyond what I thought I had by leaning on the presence of my kids. To this day, during the times I feel like quitting, I think about my kids and how I would act if they were standing right there watching me. It always pulls me through. As a father, if you're not reaching your potential—both as a father and as a person—then you will not be able to teach your children how to live a good life and how to lead others to do the same. And you will ultimately lose their respect, no matter how many times you take them to school or play video games with them.

It all begins here. With you. Act accordingly.

DEBRIEF

+ List the pathways to success that you've discovered or produced that your family members would not likely discover on their own.
+ Which of your personal attributes would you like to see in your son? Which ones would you not like to see?
+ What personal accomplishments have you produced that serve as a good example to your son?
+ What accomplishments would you like to produce in the future as an example to your son?
+ Are you someone you want your son to be like?
+ Are you the most interesting person in your son's life? Why or why not?
+ What challenges have your kids inspired you to overcome?
+ Are you in the constant practice of learning new things and remaining someone worth learning from?

+ Are you as happy and healthy as you want your son to be?
+ Does permission to live a good life so that you can lead your son to do the same inspire or scare you? Why?

3

DON'T BE RIGHT. BE EFFECTIVE.

It is a misconception that Navy SEALs see themselves as superheroes—invincible, infallible, perfect, flawless. The very first slide of the very first class on the very first day of sniper school featured this quote attributed to the Greek poet Archilochus: *We don't rise to the level of our expectations. We fall to the level of our training.* SEAL students learn, and learn quickly, that their ability to succeed is not some kind of godly power bestowed upon them but is tied directly to their very human ability to train.

You will not last long in SEAL training if you don't check your ego at the door. Humility, knowing that you don't hold all the answers or always know the best way, is at the core of being a Navy SEAL. We believe in the lifelong pursuit of knowledge and of the most effective answer. We believe in the constant quest to do better.

I meet many men who say that they want to do better, to change and achieve something greater than their current situation. However, I have met very few men who are more committed to those ambitions than they are to their current habits and comforts. Talk about chasing the bull! Can you imagine listening to someone tell you that he wants to produce more, make more money, perform better at his job, or be a better father and then see all of his actions absolutely counter that? I can, and I've often found that to be the case.

WHAT DUDES SAY	WHAT I HEAR
"I know what I'm doing."	"I'm too embarrassed or macho to ask for help."
"I'm never wrong."	"I've never tried to do anything beyond myself, and I'm certainly not going anywhere new."
"I want to improve, but (insert reason #1, reason #2, etc.)."	"I want to improve but don't want to do anything different than what I'm doing now."

Navy SEALs are undeterred by correction and committed to progressing, which means they need—and want—a mentor or teacher who will:

+ Watch them.
+ Observe where they are in their journey.
+ Report on whether they are producing the results they have promised to deliver, and how they can do better.
+ Make assessments as to what is working and what is not.

"I talk a lot about cognitive dissonance as it relates to fire-arms training. Many students who sign up for my course have learned something one way—maybe their grandfather

taught them how to shoot, and they love old Granddad— so that when I come along with my newfangled ways of shooting, even though I can show them scientifically how my method is going to work better, for some reason they will fight against it and say, 'No, that just doesn't seem right.' They won't even try to see if my way works. That's one of the hardest parts of my training—just getting people to be open to it. SEALs—and I think the majority of people do not understand this—are super-open to advice and changing and something new. We bring in experts from whatever activity we're trying to learn to do. It doesn't matter who you are, where you came from; if you can do it better than we can, then we are all ears."

—CHRIS SAJNOG, RETIRED NAVY SEAL

Mentors are everywhere if you look for them. Proven business performers, fathers, teachers, authors, and advanced education leaders exist all around us. However, not only do many of us fail to access them, but when we do, we fail to learn from them. Why?

People don't like to be wrong; nor do they like to change what they're doing. Many people just like to complain about their situation so that they can feel better about it in the moment. However, to change, to produce a different result, means that their current ways of thinking and existing habits must change.

In the military, we just can't afford to waste time on excuses. We need others to watch our back and point us in the right direction. When you're surrounded by good mentors and coaches, you develop better intuition, as well as better tactics and strategies. A commitment to being right thwarts progress. A commitment to finding the right way guides it. If a SEAL finds a better way, he'll always take it.

"Every day, I learn something new about myself. My youngest daughter recently had a tooth infection, so she was in a real 'mommy' state. One morning, when I was trying to help everybody get ready to go to the dentist, she was melting down in her room, and no matter what Papa did, nothing seemed to work. All of a sudden, that instructor in me started popping out and I caught myself saying, 'Heather, this is UNSAT!' She screamed louder, and I thought, Wow, there really is so much I don't understand about parenting. *Being aware and having the humility to recognize that is so important and critical, so that you constantly look for external influences to help you with those challenging decisions and situations, and really curtail your own emotional responses, particularly when you're dealing with toddlers."*

—**DAVID RUTHERFORD, FORMER NAVY SEAL**

OWNING UP TO YOUR MISTAKES

SEALs organize around everything they do as if in a perpetual situation of life or death. For this reason, when someone fucks up, lies, or is bullshitting himself or others, they won't hesitate to haze the shit out of one another. To change behavior for a bunch of alpha males, *talking* a bunch doesn't do it—*experiencing* consequences does. (Like me, a lot of my SEAL brothers have had some challenge in their lives or lost access to our fathers and will admit to gravitating toward the SEAL Teams because we knew we needed someone to call us on our bullshit.) Shaved heads, electric shocks to the nuts, getting roughed up—these things teach you accountability pretty quickly, and not always for offenses that are particularly egregious or dishonorable.

One day when I was serving as a sniper school instructor, we had about twenty sniper students getting their guns doped in (figuring out all of the adjustments required for a particular distance/situation) in preparation for helo (helicopter) shooting later that night. A SEAL instructor named Tommy was in charge of setting up the range so that we could quickly prepare on the 300-yard range, but we wound up spending four very frustrating hours of shooting. It was hot, and everyone was having some sort of trouble with his gun—it was like a chasing-the-bull epidemic! Multiple instructors at multiple times confirmed with Tom that we were indeed shooting at the right distance, and each inquiry appeared to drive his resolve and certainty deeper.

"Tommy, what distance are those targets?" one instructor said.

"I already told you. Three hundred," he said.

"Did you use the laser range finders?" another asked.

"Dude, I fucking told you that they're three hundred yards away."

Just before we were getting ready to shut down the range, Jake, another sniper instructor who looked and acted like a rough biker type, said, "Fuck this. Tommy, give me the fucking range finders." (Laser range finders shoot out an invisible laser beam that measures distance.)

"Why the fuck for?" Tommy asked, pissed off.

"Fucking give them to me!" said Jake, who outweighed Tommy by at least fifty pounds. After checking the laser range finders, Jake said, "Goddamn it, the targets are at four hundred yards. What the fuck?"

Tommy said nothing. It was clear that he had either measured the target distance wrong or not measured it at all. We all ended up staying a bit longer and finally got the guns doped in.

Afterward, when we were driving our trucks out, Jake,

Tommy, and I were driving together, and Jake told Tommy to close the gate to the range. Once Tommy jumped out, Jake drove the truck away and left him there, 3 miles away from camp. I remember thinking, *Fuck yeah, Jake doesn't take any shit.*

Later that night, we were drinking, and Brandon, as he does, made a smartass comment to Tommy, reminding him of the incident earlier that day. (SEALs are notorious for not letting shit drop.)

Tommy said, "Fuck you, Webb," and threw a glob of peanut butter at us.

Unamused, Brandon said, "Tommy, clean that shit up."

Again, "Fuck you, Webb."

Brandon and I dropped our heads. We knew what this meant.

After Tommy headed off to bed, we told the students to go get him and tape him up. Even though we were all SEALs, they felt a bit of reluctance because technically Tommy was their sniper instructor, but they brought him out.

Tommy tried to fight us off, but we taped up his head with riggers' tape (like duct tape), creating what we call a "happy hat" (which, since the tape sticks to your hair, is anything but). Tommy managed to break free and ran down the hall, ripping the tape off. Eventually, we caught him and added some "lobster claws" to his costume, taping up his hands. Now, with an even tighter happy hat and a set of lobster claws, we felt the point had been made. An hour or so went by before Tommy finally got all the tape off.

As far as Brandon and I were concerned, the incident was over, forgiven and forgotten, but Tommy wasn't quite there yet. In a last-ditch effort of pride and internal justice, Tommy went up to Brandon and jumped at him as if he were going to punch him. Brandon didn't even flinch and calmly said to Tommy, "Are we done here?" It was only then that Tommy finally admitted that he was in the wrong. He walked off and went to bed. It was over.

Team guys fuck up all the time. That's what happens when you're operating on the periphery and out there innovating in situations of life and death. Tommy didn't get a happy hat for fucking up. He got it for not owning the mistake the moment the possibility of it existed. He was too committed to being right. When the distance of his target was questioned, he should have said, "Oh, shit, I might have fucked that up, fellas. Let me double-check." Once he realized he was in the wrong, he could have given a sincere apology: "Damn, guys, I just wasted a bunch of your time. I won't let that happen again. I owe you all some beer." Nobody would have had a problem with that. However, if you make a mistake and try to bullshit your way out of it, there will be five dudes saying, "Shut the fuck up." You'll get hazed. You'll get beat up, not because those five dudes are assholes, but because they care enough about you to know that when you're committed more to being right than you are to being effective, that mindset has the potential to kill you—and your entire unit—out in the field.

I'm not condoning hazing or physical abuse for any of our kids. SEALs are highly trained and have a great deal of confidence, so treatment such as lobster claws and happy hats, though it sounds extreme, is not a big deal for a SEAL. Also, we're trained in prisoner-handling techniques, so we know how to safely subdue someone. You don't need to shave your son's head and pour Tabasco sauce on his pecker the next time he fucks up and doesn't own up to it. Just care enough to call out his bullshit in a way that allows him to experience the consequences of his actions. With Jason, I've always found that just the act of correcting him has been enough of a consequence.

IF YOU AIN'T CHEATIN', YOU AIN'T TRYIN'

There's an expression we like to say in the SEALs: *If you ain't cheatin', you ain't tryin'.* In combat, in unconventional warfare, this means that sometimes SEALs have to break the rules to make shit happen instead of being stuck in ineffective paradigms or limiting themselves with preconceived notions about what can and can't be done. It's about independence—not following the herd or worrying about fitting in.

TEACHING YOUR SON TO OWN UP
TO HIS MISTAKES

A few years back, I got a call from my wife, Belisa, that Jason was refusing to do his homework. As his stepmother, she had taken things as far as she thought reasonable—she told him what to do and informed him that if he didn't do it he could not play any video games or go outside—and it was now a *wait until your dad gets home* situation. Jason had always been a solid kid, so a straight refusal to do what he's told was uncommon, and it was my intent to keep it that way.

When I got home, I found Jason sitting on the stairs in quiet protest. I don't recall the exact details of what he said, but it went something like "My teachers are stupid" and "I shouldn't have to do their homework, because it's a waste of time." For all I knew, Jason might have had a stupid teacher and the homework might indeed have been a waste of time (I find that it often is), but homework needs to get done, and good grades must get produced. This, for now, was a game that Jason had to learn to play.

"Okay," I said once I was clear that he was, in fact, refusing to do as he was told. "Go get your skateboard and your PlayStation, and meet me in the backyard."

It was winter in Southern California, which doesn't seem like a big deal, but it was so cold that the antifreeze pumps for our pool had kicked on. Jason met me in the backyard and handed me his stuff. I took a deep breath and looked over at Belisa, who nodded, giving me the go-ahead. I threw Jason's PlayStation in the cold pool and smashed his skateboard against the bricks. Jason looked at me and immediately realized that although he might have been right about his homework being a waste of his time, his choice not to do it when asked might not have been as effective as he thought it would be.

"Now, get your PlayStation," I told Jason.

He reached for the pool net.

"What are you doing?" I asked.

"Getting the PlayStation," he said.

"No," I said, "go in the water and get it."

All of my kids have been brought up experiencing the consequences of the actions and situations that they cause. If left unchecked, our children can carry a commitment to being right rather than effective into adulthood and find themselves constantly making up reasons why things are the way they are or why they did or did not do something. It's our job to develop our children's ability to question their own interpretations and to pivot—without delay, guilt, or bad feelings about being wrong—the moment they discover more effective ones.

Producing cause and consequences is a skill that should be taken very seriously. It's a popular notion that any form of punishment should fit the crime—a severe consequence for a severe offense, and a mild consequence for a mild offense—but for me it's about producing results, not justice. I have a formula that has served me well:

- ✦ Safe: The consequences I produce are designed to be safe.
- ✦ Confident: The consequences are designed to maintain my children's confidence.
- ✦ Relationship: The consequences are designed to maintain our relationship.
- ✦ Effective: The consequences are designed to alter my children's behavior.

Tossing a kid's PlayStation into a pool and making him go in after it could border on abusive for many and has the potential to shatter a kid's confidence and even cause him to say he *hates* you, but Jason has spent a lifetime in the water with me, and getting sent into a cold pool isn't an overly excessive experience for him. In the end, he was safe, his confidence was maintained, our relationship actually improved, and, most important, although the *my teachers are stupid and I shouldn't have to do homework* attitude remained, his refusal to do his homework because of it went away.

FUCK UP AND OWN IT

As we discussed in chapter 2, we need to be the men we want our sons to be. Therefore, the best way to get your son to point out his mistakes is by pointing out yours. Check this out: One summer I was free-diving not far from my house in SoCal with my son when he was about seventeen. It was a sunny day, and the water was super glassy. Most divers use standard off-the-shelf flotation, but I have these cool compact James Bond–looking black pouches that attach to my dive belt—they literally have rip cords on them, much like a parachute. We were diving in deep water and very heavy kelp about 500 yards from the beach. I gave the pouches to my son so that if he got into trouble he'd be able to pull the rip cords and self-rescue; the CO_2 cartridges would inflate the air bladders and send him shooting to the safety of the surface. I explained how they worked and told him that he could count on them if he got into a potential life-or-death situation. However, I hadn't checked to see if the CO_2 cartridges were in the pouches. It was only after the dive was over and I was cleaning them out that I realized they weren't.

I told him, "I was wrong for not checking, and you could've died because of that. I messed up."

He looked up at me and asked why I called myself out like that.

"Because, buddy," I said proudly, "I don't care about being right. I only care about being effective. Now you know that I can fuck up something like this, and moving forward you'll know to double-check my work as well as the work of others when your life is on the line."

That's the kind of accountability that SEALs have, and that's the kind of accountability I want to teach my son or any of my kids. No one's going to trust me if I try to hide shit. Men need to stop trying to hide and cover up their flaws and mistakes, because when they do they're only teaching their sons that being right is more important than being *real*. They're also teaching them that they can't be trusted.

Even at the age of forty-three, I find myself drifting toward a propensity of blaming Belisa for things that go wrong around the house or with the kids. I can't think of anything less manly than screwing something up and then blaming the one who supports you the most for the things that were ultimately your fault. Sometimes I fear that it's only a matter of time before I'm pulled out of my bed and taped up by her, and with good cause. I remind myself that a point man isn't leading his platoon to their objective when he's walking in the wrong direction. He's leading them only after he realizes that he's gone the wrong way and turns around. Fuck up and own it. You'll grow, and others will trust you.

> "Eric's saving grace will always be that he recognizes when he is screwing up and when he misplaces blame. It may take a day or two before he realizes it, but he always does. With age, he recognizes it earlier than he used to. He isn't afraid to say 'I'm sorry' or admit that he ultimately is to blame. As hard as it is to be the one being blamed, I also understand that it isn't me with whom he is upset. He is upset with himself and with the outcome of the situation. In the end, he will always take full responsibility even when it isn't his fault, which can be equally as frustrating. It isn't all his responsibility, but he takes his role as leader of our family so seriously that everything can be, or is, a life-or-death situation for him. When you move that way in life, mistakes are harder to take. As the person closest to him and as his partner, I will be the one he looks to first, because it is always easier to look outward than inward for most of us. I know he gets upset, because we are so deliberate in the choices we are making for our family that it is hard when it doesn't go the way we wanted it to, so that it isn't a personal attack on me even when it feels like it is. Plus, if he didn't apologize I would have wrapped him up in duct tape and tasered him a long time ago. I don't have time for that behavior."
>
> **—BELISA DAVIS**

WHAT'S FAIRNESS GOT TO DO WITH IT?

What is fairness? An equal playing field? A state or condition free of bias or prejudice? It simply doesn't exist, and those who think of fairness as an inherent human right will, no doubt, be disappointed. Fairness is a powerful and useful notion that allows groups of people to function in a trusting and predictable manner within the rules of their game or agreement. However, outside of an agreed-upon and cooperative relationship, fairness becomes a subjective and personal expectation of how things should have gone or people should have acted. Life's not always fair and if we don't learn how to deal with that, unfairness can chew us up.

In SEAL training, if your buddy is performing at a subpar level, you have to make up for it. It could potentially be unfair if your swim buddy wasn't taking care of himself or got tired. I remember one instance when my swim buddy and I desperately had to pass a 2-mile timed ocean swim. I was so amped and ready that I just took off. My swim buddy couldn't keep up with me. I just grabbed him and pulled. In SEAL training, leaving your swim buddy behind would end your career immediately. When you're new and arrogant, you'll feel like this holds you back, but since your instructors force the relationship to always stay intact, you eventually have the opportunity to see that it's an overall gain even if there are some temporary setbacks.

As my swim buddy struggled to keep up with me, I remember thinking that between the two of us, we needed to deliver a 100 percent passing swim—it didn't matter if I carried 99 percent and he carried 1 percent, or the other way around. One way or the other, *him plus me* had to equal a passed swim. If you want to see a SEAL instructor come unglued, try telling him that you failed something because of your swim buddy. I watched a guy try that once only to find himself immediately isolated from the class and hammered until he quit.

TURNING NEGATIVE SELVES INTO A POSITIVE

As a society we think being self-sufficient is a good thing; in fact, there is nothing we do for which, at some point, we didn't receive help. After I left the Teams, I had an opportunity to study with two amazing teachers, Toby Hecht and Greg Scharnagl of the Aji Network, who taught me that there are three types of people in the world.

+ **Plus Selves:** Those who are arrogant and fail because they think they don't need help.
+ **Zero Selves:** Those who think they can take help or leave it.
+ **Negative Selves:** Those who know that they, by themselves, are not sufficient, so they get really good at getting help. These are the successful ones.

Therefore, when my kids need help with math or a subject in which I'm not proficient, I teach them how to get it. I show them how to conduct online searches or how to reach out and build networks of help. Navy SEALs are often described as arrogant, because we believe that we can do anything. The reason we believe this is because we literally *can* do anything. At our core, we are negative selves and have become very good at getting good help. As Toby and Greg taught me, it doesn't have to be *your* body that gets it done.

Sometimes, to speed things up during PT, the instructors would have one of our IBSs (inflatable small boats) filled up with cold water so that when someone performed below standards they could just send him to the boat to get wet rather than waiting for him to run out to the ocean and back. (They're efficient like that.) We were just a few weeks into First Phase, still pre–Hell Week, when one of the instructors told some other boat crew to have two boats ready for the next morning's PT. To this day, I'm not sure how this is even possible, but when we showed up for PT the next morning there were no boats. Somebody forgot.

"Where are the boats?" Instructor Samuels asked.

Blank stares.

"Who'd I tell to have the boats ready for PT?" he asked.

Awkward silence.

"Yesterday, I was standing right by those poles, and I told someone to have the boats ready for PT this morning. Who was it?"

A quiet *"Hooyah"* came from behind me, simultaneously meaning *Yes, that was me* and *Holy fucking shit, I can't believe this is about to happen.*

"Push-ups," Instructor Samuels said. "Begin, one, two, three . . ."

The guy didn't say a word about the boats. He just started the workout.

Him not saying a word about the boats was the worst possible thing that could have happened because we all knew that there was no way in hell that a SEAL instructor would allow a blatant disregard for instructions to go unaddressed. The best-case scenario, and the most common, would have been for the guilty party to go hit the surf, but clearly the infraction had warranted a response that would take some time to think about. In this case it took some time to coordinate.

The instructors decided to make an example out of the forgetful boat crew and scheduled a special remediation for them that night. That was the reason nothing happened right away—Instructor Samuels needed to see if some other instructors were available to come in that night to collectively hammer the offenders. Apparently, they had no other plans. The remediation was on.

As the day progressed, the instructors decided to make the most of their time and include other boat crews who had previously registered performance shortfalls. We were all on high alert and extra careful to make sure that we did everything right. My boat crew was solid, so I wasn't worried. Then, near the end of the day, we just happened to run by Instructor Samuels, who said something like "Hey, you guys look like a pack of monkeys trying to fuck a football bat. Show up tonight for remediation." We collectively replied, *"Hooyah,"* and went on about the rest of our day, thinking, *Oh well, just another night of hitting the surf,* but we were wrong. The night would be exceptional, but not in a good way.

Wheelbarrow carries in the soft sand. Push-ups. Deep leg lunges. Beating our boots—standing, squatting, slapping our boots, standing back up, squatting, etc.—for hours. We did monkey fuckers—squatting down, holding on to our ankles, and then squatting up and down, up and down—until our legs were on fire and we could barely stand. The leg lunges, monkey fuckers, buddy carries, trips to the surf—they kept going, and I thought, *Holy shit, we still have tomorrow to do.* It got very real very quickly. My legs were done.

I remember running to the surf and seeing a classmate of mine in shorts and flip-flops. He had just gotten back from eating his second dinner (you eat dinner as a class in the chow hall at the end of the day, but you burn so many calories in the day you end up going out to eat again at night). He was just smiling at us, and that's when it hit me: *Dude, this is so unfair.* We were in the same SEAL class, in the same phase of training, and there he was—fat, dumb, and happy while I was getting my ass handed to me because I happened to run by someone at the wrong time. There was no real reason for me not to be standing right there with him holding my leftovers from my second dinner. This was some bullshit now.

The next day, we were nearly crippled. Dudes started quitting left and right. Most of us could barely move, much less finish an evolution to standard. Some of the instructors didn't even know what had happened to us the night before. We just looked like we were sandbagging.

"Davis! Why are you so far behind the rest of the class?"

You didn't dare break into an explanation, as it would only be taken as an excuse, a lack of personal responsibility. *"Hooyah,"* I replied with a smile on my face, meaning *Because I got my ass handed to me last night and now I'm not strong enough to keep up, but I'm not going to say a word.* I had accepted that SEAL training was, as it should be, not fair, and the only real reason for me falling behind the next day was that I was not strong enough to keep up. Period.

I have no doubt that the reason guys quit the next day was because it was all so unfair. There was no reason for the hammering, and it wasn't something the entire class had gone through. They just couldn't take the injustice. They were right when they said, "This is some bullshit." They just weren't effective in be-coming a SEAL.

We had randomly run by the instructor. We could have run the other way, but we didn't. It was just one of those things. The rules changed from *Don't screw up and everything will be fine* to *Run by the wrong instructor and you're fucked.* When you're a team, as a family is, you shouldn't care who is in the wrong or dropping the ball in the moment. You'll step up and gladly fill in. You'll pivot, as we discussed in chapter 1. In the long game, problem solving doesn't mean getting stuck on blame or feel-ing sorry for yourself or bemoaning the unfairness of it all. It means remaining focused on the desired outcome and getting shit done.

There's an entire generation of young adults out there right now acting entitled and demanding fairness in every situation in which they participate. I'm watching organizations struggle to accommodate them by trying to make things "fair." This will never work, because life isn't fair. Our enemies or business com-petitors don't care about what's fair; they care about what works for them. This entire generation is about to get bitch-slapped by those who are willing to work and make things happen even if their lunch hour gets cut short or they have to stay late to get the job done. Will it be *right* that people from other countries took their jobs? Perhaps not, but it will be *effective* for the businesses and their customers.

Men, our sons are going to experience unfair challenges and get hit with anything from an illness to an injury. They're going to have to learn to deal with teachers who have checked out, un-fair grading, school elections, dances, shitty friends, dating, and jobs that should have gone to them but went to someone else. If you thought the world seemed unfair as a kid, just wait until you see how unfair it is when you're a father. Our sons need to be ready. And so do we.

"One of the greatest lessons that my dad taught me was not what to know but how to learn. One of his big lessons was the necessity of asking why. That became a core way for me to experience the world. My father was a lawyer, and his advice was always to enter a conversation with the assumption that you are wrong and that the person with the differing opinion or answer is right. Therefore, throughout that conversation, it is up to you to continue to ask questions until you prove either that you were right and the other person was wrong, or that the other person was right, so you can adopt a new, more effective perspective. The key to finding those answers is to ask why at least twice and how at least once. When you do this, you discover the power of inquiry. Most people don't know why or how. They have no clue why they think what they do. Because someone told me. Because it makes sense. *Yes, but why does it make sense? If you don't know, then your answer shouldn't be* I don't know *or* Leave me alone *but* How can we find out? Where can we find that information? Whom can we ask? *If someone has a more effective way of doing something, you need to start using it. As a parent, when your son asks why for the hundredth time, don't get frustrated. Empower him by answering again, or better yet by showing him how to get the answer himself."*

—LARRY YATCH, RETIRED NAVY SEAL

LARRY YATCH: SAFETY IN NUMBERS

Larry Yatch, a graduate of the U.S. Naval Academy, spent ten years, from 1998 to 2008, as an officer in the Navy SEAL Teams. He has received many awards, including the Navy and Marine Corps Commendation Medal with a Combat "V" for valor, the Achievement Medal for innovation in SEAL combat tactics, the Global War on Terrorism Expeditionary Medal, and the Humanitarian Service Medal for relief efforts in East Timor and Sri Lanka. His service to his country ended when he was severely injured in the line of duty and medically retired from the Navy SEALs. In 2008, Yatch, with his wife, Anne, started Sealed Mindset, a Navy SEAL–inspired defense-training center that trains thousands of citizens in the art of threat identification, avoidance, deterrence, and defense, and offers a variety of tools, training, and inspiration to grow confidence and overcome personal challenges. The Yatches then founded Mindset Matters, an innovative curriculum company that brings critical lessons on leadership and personal safety to youth across the country. Finally, the Yatches created Sealed Mindset Leaders to bring the uncommon Navy SEAL leadership mindsets, structures, and knowledge to companies and organizations. Yatch has a two-year-old son, Colt.

A large part of my business centers on teaching people how to be safe, and we get a large number of parents who have college-aged children who come in and say, "I'm concerned for my high school seniors who are going off to college. They don't know how to take care of themselves. Do you have a program for them?"

"Yes," I tell them, "we have a college safety course that you can attend with your children."

"Well, I don't have time for that" is what I usually hear. "I just want something for them."

"Do you know how to take care of yourself?" I ask.

"Well," they say, "not really."

And there lies the root of the problem.

I'm always amazed when people expect their children to have a skill that they have no interest in learning. Did these parents teach their children manners by sending them to a four-hour course on manners and then eat like a slob every time they were around them? Probably not. They might have showed them a YouTube video on manners and talked about it, but more than anything they ate with manners, modeling the behavior they wanted to pass on. Keeping their children safe is no different. If they can't show them how to take care of themselves, if they themselves don't know how to identify bad situations and take actions to avoid conflict, how can they expect their children to do it? Based on that mentality, and the way they operate and move through the world, they're just ripe for the picking, and they are modeling behavior that will make their children vulnerable.

In my own family, my wife and I do not tolerate a victim mentality. It's not the way our family does business. We have standards not unlike those that are taught in the SEALs, certain codes of behavior that our son will need to have and that are a part of our family culture. Therefore, Colt will have to learn how to defend himself just as we expect him to treat people politely. For us, it's just a way of being.

It will start with us modeling certain behaviors that the SEAL Teams have used for years to remain safe in some of the world's worst environments. We are always aware of our surroundings when we are in an uncontrolled environment. Colt will see us assessing everything around us as threats, possible threats, or nonthreats in a relaxed, almost subconscious manner. We will teach him how to take immediate action if we are ever presented with a threat to our safety, and these actions will be standard and practiced: create distance, introduce a barricade, look for avenues of escape or help, and finally, as a last resort, defend ourselves. He will learn to embody a warrior's spirit when it is time for defense, one in which we fight hard, we never quit, and we never lose.

DEBRIEF

+ What parenting paradigms have you found to be irrelevant or ineffective?
+ Who are you currently being coached or trained by? How does it relate to your role as a father?
+ Name at least one ineffective parenting technique you've used or are using. How will you change it?
+ When have you disciplined your son in a way that would be considered "right," but you found it to be ineffective?
+ When you're in the wrong, do you own up to it and call yourself out or hide it?
+ Are you humble and good at getting help, or arrogant and think you can do everything yourself?

- Give an example of a time you taught your son how to get good help.
- Give an example of a time you were able to truly help your son see things for what they were and not what he wanted them to be.

4

IT'S EASIER TO KEEP UP THAN CATCH UP

In SEAL training, when you fall behind on a physical evolution, such as running, you are put into what's called the Goon Squad. The instructors immediately gather this group of guys, who are tired and, most likely, dry-heaving at this point, not to let them rest but to drop the hammer and increase the duration and intensity of the evolution—push-ups, trips into the cold Pacific, buddy carries, endless sprints, and bear crawls until they puke or until the instructor staff is satisfied that they've learned their lesson.

What lesson?

That they're capable of more than they realize.

SEAL students learn something powerful when they find themselves in the Goon Squad—they discover how much more they can take, how much more they have left in them, in secret reserves that were even secret to them. Many times, guys fall behind in SEAL training because they think they lack endurance or aren't fast enough, but the Goon Squad, with the immediate demand for more, shows them that they could have handled what had been thrown at them simply because they're handling so much more now. There's a powerful lesson there. When you realize that you are physically able to do sprints on the beach for an hour immediately after the run in which you fell behind, it is a clear and present indicator that you didn't dig deep enough the first time, that you could have kept up with your class after all and avoided the extra pain and mileage. It's for this reason that we say in the SEAL teams: *It's easier to keep up than catch up.*

SINK OR SWIM

During a water-treading exercise in SEAL training, this small Asian kid started gasping. Concerned, the instructors asked, "Are you having problems?" The kid acknowledged that he was in trouble by choking out, "Yes, can't breathe, I can't do this." One of the instructors held out his hand—"Here, take this"—and it wasn't until the kid reached out to grab the object that he realized it was a dive brick (a rubberized, weighted brick used for underwater work), which, as soon as he held it, led him straight to the bottom of the pool. Fifteen seconds later, the kid blacked out and had to be rescued by the corpsmen. I've blacked out twice during underwater swims. To truly learn how much you have left in you, sometimes you have to take things to the limit. From that day on, I'm sure that Asian kid knew with total confidence where *enough* stopped and *too much* started. Unfortunately for him, SEAL training became *too much.*

RUDDER CORRECTIONS

For a lot of us, *keeping up* is something we struggle with every day—work, family, living a healthy lifestyle. And much the way it happens in SEAL training, when we fall behind, life tends to drop the hammer on us even more.

+ You fall behind on bills and then get slapped with fees, adding even more to what you owe.
+ Your son's teacher has been leaving phone messages for you, but you can't find the time to return the calls. When you finally do, you discover that it's too late; your son has flunked the course.
+ You've spent the first fifteen years of your daughter's life too busy to form a relationship, and when she has boy troubles and you offer to help, she wants nothing to do with you.

The only way to keep the extra hammering at bay is by continually staying the course. Life—not unlike airplanes, ships, and other vessels—is off course 99 percent of the time. Therefore, fathers—not unlike pilots, captains, and *leaders*—need to make adjustments as they go. Think about when you drive an automobile down the street. You don't plant your hands at ten and two, keep the steering wheel rigidly straight, and hope for the best; you move the wheel slightly to the left or right, depending upon which way the vehicle begins to veer. As parents, we must react to input, whether it comes from a compass, a speedometer, team members, or unknown elements, so that we can keep from drifting farther off course. There is no cruise control in parenting. In the navy, we call these *rudder corrections*. Can you imagine a pilot or a ship's captain throwing up his hands every time his navigation equipment indicated he was drifting? He'd sail in circles, which is what we all do when we resist change. It is our job as parents to provide our children with consistent rudder corrections, redefining their limits and reorganizing their efforts, because if we don't it will take that much more time and energy after they drift away to get them where they want to go.

ALWAYS SAY YES

Parents have developed a nasty habit of telling their children no all the time. They tell themselves that they should say no because they don't want to spoil their kids, but the truth is that it's often because they're too tired or lazy to say yes, so they come up with bullshit reasons for saying no—"it's too dangerous," "it's too late," "it's too far away," "I'm too busy," anything that will solve the immediate problem, which is that they don't want, or don't have the time, to give the request much thought. They don't want to *keep up* with what's going on. For that reason, kids may become frustrated and disrespectful with lazy parents who constantly take the easy "no" road. They know damn well that there's no reason why they can't go to their friend's house or stay outside for another hour or two. And so do their parents.

INSISTENT AND CONSISTENT

Keeping up seems easy enough, but many parents don't do it. They have a habit of storing their parenting energy in reserve for the times when they think their kids need them most—behavior issues, bad grades, talking back, extremely poor decisions. Yet parenting is a 'round-the-clock responsibility. Stepping in only when an offense or issue has forced our parenting hand into action is not only ineffective in the long term but will cause our kids to lose respect for us as they become used to getting along without us. They think, *Who the fuck is this guy and why is he showing up now?* It's important that we maintain consistency in our parenting and that we parent in real time, so that when the teachable moments show up, we're ready and willing to teach our kids, and our kids are ready and willing to learn. If we fall too far behind, we'll end up in the Goon Squad and either have to work to reestablish the relationship or, if things get really bad, find ourselves in a situation where we don't have the juice left to keep up. We can lose the pack permanently if we're not careful.

Training my Belgian Malinois, Indy, helped me realize that I was no longer keeping up with my kids and gave me new knowledge and awareness as to what I could and should be doing with them. As a result, I pulled back from Indy's training, working with her only occasionally, so I could focus on my kids, and that began to have a negative effect on my relationship with Indy. One day, I was in the field with her doing bite work and trying to "turn the training on," but she was jittery and wasn't behaving. I started correcting her for every command that in the past she would respond to and perform flawlessly. For example, I wanted her to stay by my side, but she wanted to charge the dude with the bite sleeve. Or, once she was on the bite and I wanted her to come off, she got indignant—I could see her aggression tune up, as her eyes were now looking to me with suspicion rather than confirmation. We were no longer a "dog team"; she was a dog, and I was some dickhead yanking her leash. The entire session ended up being a huge failure as she continued to do the doggy version of panic. It was a complete abortion, and it cost me thousands of dollars and much time to repair the damage caused by not keeping up with her.

At the time I was angry, frustrated, and disappointed with Indy, which is a trip because she probably wanted to do nothing but please me. I mean, a teenager can fool you into thinking that he really does want to be miserable, but a dog? Not a chance. I had been inconsistent in my training, which led to a confused dog. (If you keep that inconsistency up, smart and confident dogs will eventually turn around and bite your ass. If they've been raised right, they won't take shit from anybody.) I had to make sure not to let that happen again; I had to be able to keep up with raising my kids *and* my dog training, as an engaged father should.

When we choose to parent only when we have the energy or inclination, the inconsistency confuses our kids. When we tolerate behaviors at some times and not others, they see us as this unstable entity that cannot predictably be satisfied; any attempt to live by our rules will only frustrate us and hurt them, and then the only times we parent become negative experiences. That's the last thing we want, since our children are sure to have enough negative experiences *out there*. They need us to provide a safe haven, where leadership is consistent and makes sense.

COACHING, NOT CORRECTING

When I was twelve years old, I was standing at the plate when the pitcher let the ball go. I could see it coming almost in slow motion and heading right toward me, but for whatever reason I couldn't seem to move. *Thud.* The ball slammed into my left side, just above my hip.

TENETS OF A GOOD COACH

Coaching is a skill. It takes practice to do it well. It wasn't until I got into the military that I finally had good coaches and became a part of an institution that had had hundreds of years to evolve and create an environment where individuals could excel. No longer was I being coached by the unqualified. Some of the best coaches know how to:

+ Observe behavior without judging it.
+ Change behavior in a way that builds confidence.
+ Push you without breaking you.
+ Remain organized to keep you progressing down a consistent path.
+ Read you and know where you are, both emotionally and physically.
+ Communicate clear end states.
+ Remain curious rather than certain.
+ Remain relevant by being in constant study.
+ Love their students and accept them for who they are, so that they can help them become who they can be.
+ Approach coaching as the ultimate responsibility and opportunity to change the lives of those they coach.

Start practicing now.

My coach, an older, kind of crusty guy, said nothing. The next time I was at bat, the pitch came and it took everything in me not to dive into the dirt. *Strike one.* This happened two more times, and each time my coach yelled, "Davis, what are you doing? Swing at the ball. Don't be afraid of it." I became embarrassed and could feel everyone watching me.

In the same game, I was playing outfield, and the ball came sailing toward me. I had practiced so much in the grass behind my townhouse that I could actually dive into the air, catch the ball, and land on the back of my head and summersault my way through the play, but this time, when the ball was headed my way all I could think about was the coach getting mad at me if I tried to dive and missed it. Instead, I held back and let the ball take a bounce before it landed in my glove.

At the end of that inning, as I made my way back to the dugout, the coach walked out to me and said, "Why in the hell didn't you dive for that ball? Now go get in the dugout, and try not to be scared of the ball anymore." This coach did not know how to change the behavior of a twelve-year-old without breaking his confidence, and after that season and nearly seven consecutive years of playing baseball, I never played again.

When I got to high school, I had a similar experience. I tried out for the football team and made it as a second-string tight end, which was great because I had never played football before. During one pivotal game, the coach yelled, "I need another tight end to go in after this play." I started to get my helmet on, and he glanced at me and looked away. "I need a tight end to go in after this play. Someone's got to go in. Who's it going to be?"

I was devastated. He knew that it was my position, and he was intentionally going to send in someone else—anyone else but me. After that season, I never played football again.

"People often say to my two boys, 'Oh, are you going to be just like your dad, the Navy SEAL?' And I feel like that puts them in a really tough spot. I don't care if they're a SEAL or not. I want them to be whoever they want to be, and so as a parent, I'm very careful about the types of people who associate with my boys, whether they are soccer coaches, baseball coaches, or teachers. It's incredibly important that they are surrounded by people who let them become who they need to be and promote a positive environment in which for them to learn and grow."

—BRANDON WEBB, FORMER NAVY SEAL

When children are rejected in harsh ways, their confidence can be broken, particularly when there isn't a father figure around to counter whatever negative forces are working against them. Around this time, my dad had begun to struggle with mental illness, a struggle that would come to a head as I turned sixteen. When I look back at my sports years, I always wished my dad had pushed me and guided my choices more, since he had been such a crucial role model in my early years, but it wasn't meant to be, nor was my professional sports career. When you are not leading from the front, outside forces—coaches, teachers, and other mentors— can have more time with, and a greater influence on, your kids than you do. You need to be the loudest voice in your son's head. If your son's coach sucks and looks as if he has the potential to ruin what should be a positive experience, you have various options:

+ Modify your son's experience by talking with him and teaching him how to deal with idiot coaches.
+ Modify the environment by talking with the coach.
+ Modify the environment by becoming an assistant coach.

LEARN. PRACTICE. EXPERIENCE. REPEAT.

Learning comes down to repetition, and for learning to be effective and efficient, your repetition must also be effective and efficient. My children will be the first to tell you, "Dad covers so much stuff with me I can barely keep up," and I'll often get teased by them or their mother that I try to teach them more than they can hold, but what I'm doing is intentional. High-level learning requires four phases.

Learn: Learning is gathering sufficient information about something and then organizing it into a specific sequence, so that the sequence can accurately be repeated (practiced) and will eventually produce a desired result. Learning is achieved through carefully organized research, study, and meticulous note taking. Often when we fail to develop a skill it's because there was a flaw in our learning phase.

Practice: Practice is taking what we learned and repeating it until we can consistently and on demand produce the desired result. Our practice can only be as good as our learning. We learn how to shoot a sniper rifle—ballistics, body position, trigger squeeze, how the scope works—and then we perfectly practice each one of those things, in sequence, until they become our default behavior and we can consistently hit our targets. The same practice can also be applied to producing relationships, dealing with a bully, or showing people that we love them. We're not stuck in our default behaviors.

Experience: This is going live, deploying the skill we've learned and practiced in the environment in which we intend to use it. This produces results that can be compared and contrasted against desired outcomes. It also reveals unnoticed areas of performance that are contributing to, or detracting from, accomplishing the specific task at hand, such as not having enough time, being disorganized, or realizing that a teacher doesn't have the knowledge we need.

Repeat: Now it's time to get after it. Learn. Practice. Experience. Repeat as necessary.

+ Pluck your son from the environment if you can't make it produce the outcomes you are after.
+ If it hadn't been for my time in the SEAL Teams, I'd no doubt be some slightly older version of that twelve-year-old who had his confidence busted by shitty coaches. Since those days, I've developed an ability to get coached by even the nastiest of people. Nobody's coaching style can take my confidence away from me now.

Many teaching or coaching offers out there are selling the idea of being able to do something—become a better shooter, runner, athlete, student. It's important that you know what good coaching and training looks like, so that you can teach your son and fill in the gaps for him. As a father, I've been a close observer of my kids' coaches and have worked closely with Belisa and Stacey to make sure that we're there, filling in the gaps and making the rudder corrections, to fill the holes that insufficient coaches leave or sometimes create. I spent several years coaching each of my kids' soccer teams to ensure that they learned what good coaching looks like. As a result, my kids are extremely coachable and have powerful levels of self-confidence that help them learn and modify their choices to better move them toward their goals.

> *"Because my dad was a SEAL, his parenting style was more relaxed, but strict at the same time. For example, if homework needed to be done, we had freedom to do it when we wanted to, for the most part, but if we abused that freedom, it would not be fun. Or if we had to complete something, like swimming, in a certain amount of time, if we did not make it, we would go again, exhausted, until we got that score."*
>
> **—JASON DAVIS**

SMALL, CONTINUOUS VICTORIES

We have been trained to believe that parenting victories come when our kids don't do drugs, don't skip school, or don't get themselves knocked up. No doubt these are important, but the true victories went virtually unnoticed and happened over time, when you coached your kids through obstacles or moved their rudders to help them steer past some potentially hazardous waters. Every time you gave your children input, that input modified their lives: an answer to a question they asked you after school; a pat on the back after a difficult defeat; trying to help them solve a math homework problem, even if your math skills are a bit rusty. When our children see us making the effort to keep up with them, we not only earn their respect, but it can inspire them to do the same—stay on top of their responsibilities. I know life is hard, and we've all got stuff to do, but your sons should be your top priority. I know we can feel depleted, but chances are you've got something left in the tank. And if you've fallen behind, dig deep, sprint hard, and catch up before you get Goon Squaded.

BRANDON WEBB: THE DREAM STEALERS

After leaving home at age sixteen, Brandon Webb finished high school and joined the U.S. Navy to become a Navy SEAL. He served with SEAL Team 3, Naval Special Warfare Group 1 Training Detachment sniper cell, and completed his last tour at the Naval Special Warfare Center sniper course, where he served as the West Coast sniper course manager. Throughout his career, Brandon completed multiple deployments to the Middle East and one to Afghanistan. He would go back to Iraq in 2006–7 as a paramilitary contractor. He has received numerous distinguished service awards including the Presidential Unit Citation (personally awarded to him by President George W. Bush) and the Navy and Marine Corps Commendation medal with "V" device for valor in combat. Webb ended his navy career early after over a decade of service in order to spend more time with his children. He has two sons and a daughter, ages thirteen, twelve, and nine.

Today, Brandon is focused on pursuing his career in media and as a bestselling author. He is the founder and CEO of Force12 Media, a digital publishing company that reaches tens of millions monthly and is the largest military content network on the Internet. In 2012, he founded the Red Circle Foundation (named after his bestselling memoir), a nonprofit organization focused on supporting families of the Special Operations community through emergency memorial, medical, and child-enrichment-program (camps and scholarships) funding.

When the kids' mother and I got divorced (we're still really close), my boys moved with my ex-wife four counties away so that they could be closer to her parents. My oldest, Jackson, who was eleven years old at the time, had just started playing baseball, so I went to a game to watch him play, but he sat on the bench—visibly upset—for the entire game. After the game was over, I went right up to the coach.

"What's the problem?" I asked. "What's going on here?"

"Jackson's missed the last few practices," he said.

"That's not his fault," I said. "His mom just moved up here."

"I thought he was probably too busy playing video games," the coach said.

I wanted to rip this guy's head off. I mean, how are you going to punish an eleven-year-old boy for missing practice when it's his mom who didn't get him there on time due to a demanding mom schedule? You're just going to bench him for the whole game?

It was during moments like this that I realized how much my co-parent and I needed to watch who we let around our kids. I call people like this *dream stealers.* I say to my kids, "Look, you have to watch out for these people, and there are a lot of them out there—negative, unconstructive, unenthusiastic people. You just have to learn how to accept it, deal with it, and develop your own coping tools, and you'll be a better person for it."

Unfortunately, at that time, it was too late. Jackson became completely sour on baseball after that (he took up soccer, thankfully), and that sucked, because I loved baseball as a kid, and he didn't get a chance to develop a passion for it like I did. His mom and I removed Jackson from that environment immediately. I didn't want him to be around that guy. He wasn't a very good coach. To be honest, he wasn't a very good person, and I reported him to the league.

There is tremendous power in a positive environment. When Eric and I worked to radically redesign the SEAL sniper course, we wanted to make sure that the instructors were using positive reinforcement, and we found that—with the course standards remaining the same—the instructors were teaching better, and the students were learning better, and we started graduating more students. Before the change, we had an average attrition rate of about 30 percent. By the time we had gone through most of the overhaul, it had plummeted to less than 5 percent.

If you're trying to be a better shooter—or a better baseball player or a better anything—you have to believe it's achievable, that you can get there through hard work, practice, and perfect mental rehearsal. That's a lesson that can be applied to all areas of life, so I'm really, really careful about how I talk to my children and constantly check in with them on how they're talking to themselves and how they're being talked to. I have seen lots of crappy teachers and coaches, and I just refuse to let my kids be surrounded by them.

DEBRIEF

+ Are there any areas of your son's life—school, friends, employment—in which you've fallen behind?
+ What coaches are influencing your children besides you?
+ Are there any areas of your son's life—school, friends, employment, discipline, relationships—in which you've fallen behind?
+ How consistent are you with your parenting?
+ How good at accepting correction or discipline is your son? How does your consistency as a father affect this?

5

HESITATION KILLS

In the months preceding Operation Iraqi Freedom, my platoon was operating out of Kuwait conducting VBSS (Visit, Board, Search, and Seizure), which is best described as legal pirating.

With black hoods covering our faces and armed with nothing more than lightweight submachine guns, a pistol, and a knife, we made it a nightly practice to quietly sneak onto and seize the enemy ships who were defying the sanctions set forth by the United Nations and trying to slip out of Iraqi waters under the cover of darkness laden with contraband. Just two years prior, I had been part of a small team that conducted one of the first takedowns of this type in the region. It was quick and without resistance, because the smugglers had been operating unchecked and were unaware that the sanctions would be enforced. This time, however, things were different. They were ready for us.

With years of opposition, the smugglers had become hardened and sophisticated, and their defensive tactics and strategies were becoming more offensive and dangerous. Our entire platoon had moved from Camp Doha, a large army base located west of Kuwait City, to a naval amphibious assault ship patrolling the northern tip of the Persian Gulf.

As the platoon's sniper and head of the intelligence department, I was present for many of the situation briefs relating to all of the boarding operations or attempts in our area of operation. After lunch one day, we were called into the Operations Room and briefed on a particularly large and hard target that one of our allies had already attempted to take down.

"They've emplaced aggressive and dangerous counterboarding measures along their rails," our task unit commander, who looked like a manlier version of Tom Selleck and, no shit, went by the name Heavy P, told us. "A French team got on, but they were not able to take the bridge, so they left."

"Wait, they got on the ship and couldn't get in, so they just left?" I asked jokingly.

Heavy P took a deep breath. "Yep," he said, "they just left. They got off and went home, and the ship got away."

My buddy Larry Yatch chuckled. "Fuck that," he said. "Send us. We'll take it down. *Just left* my ass."

"You'll get your chance," Heavy P promised. "The moment they show back up on our radar. Get some sleep. We'll let you know."

Later that night, we were all racked out on the ship, sleeping soundly in these coffinlike beds stacked five high deep within the ship's bowels, when the lights came on and someone said, "It's on. They found the ship. We're leaving in ten minutes."

Still half asleep, we grabbed our gear and made our way onto the helos that were already spinning their blades in anticipation of our arrival.

By far, my preferred method of insertion was to quietly approach these ships on our 11-meter RHIBs (rigid-hull inflatable boats). Boarding from the water would allow me, as the lead climber, to send a titanium grappling hook up to the rail and then quickly scale the small caving ladder affixed to it without anyone on the ship knowing we were there. We held the element of surprise this way, but on this night they had the advantage. They already had a head start.

As soon as the target ship broke loose from the mouth of its protected Iraqi river safe haven and into the Gulf, it shot straight for Iran. This way, if the slick oil that was poured on the edge of its decks in hopes of getting us to slip off and into the dark waters below, or the wires the smugglers spread across its antennas in an effort to snag our ropes should we come from the air, failed to stop us, they would drag us into Iranian waters, which had the potential to put our platoon and our country in a very serious situation with Iran.

The helos went in low and fast, and just before they got to the enemy ship, they flared hard to get us into position. The target ship aggressively swerved in an effort to stop us.

Ben, our HRST (Helicopter Rope Suspension Training) master, spotted something unsavory on the roof of the bridge and immediately made the call to move the insertion to the bow of the boat. (The bow was a much riskier spot for us, as it moved our entire insert, the most vulnerable part of the mission, directly in front of the bridge, where we could easily be seen by anyone on the ship.) At this point, the smugglers knew a boarding was imminent, so they stopped swerving and made a beeline straight for Iran, turning the target ship full speed ahead toward the safety of the Iranian waters. The clock was ticking.

Ben kicked the ropes out of the bird and sent the platoon sliding onto the ship like firefighters down a pole. I remember the rope was at an angle by the time my turn came, forcing me to exit the helicopter, which was at least 50 feet off the deck, before I had the rope in my hands. The saying "Hesitation kills" flashed through my mind. There was no time to think, and I just kept going—out the door, into the air, and onto the rope. Exiting a helicopter with over sixty pounds of gear and bullets strapped to your body without positive contact with the rope is easily one of the worst feelings in the world.

We snaked our way to the bridge to find the doors heavily re-inforced. We quickly made our way up and around to the roof of the bridge, an easy 90 feet above the lower decks, and we had no other entry point available than through the front windows, which were also barricaded with steel slats. These guys had thought of everything.

Anticipating this contingency, Larry had already invented a method of entry: He and I would rappel over the bridge, where I would blow a hole in the glass, toss in a concussion grenade, and hold the bridge crew at gunpoint while Larry cut through the iron bars with his quickie saw. We were only minutes away from Iranian waters. We'd have to execute Larry's entry plan flawlessly in order to get in and turn the ship before we created a major inter-national incident.

Enter Murphy's Law.

One of Larry's backup ropes became tangled and inoperable. Because of the showering flames that the quickie saw would pro-duce while cutting, it was critical to use two ropes since at least one of them melting away was more likely than not. In fact, the plan was to cut until we lost a rope and stop only then.

I looked up to Ben, who was on the top of the bridge, with a stunned expression.

"Let's go," Larry said as he slipped over the edge with a single rope tied to his harness.

"Fuck it, I guess it's a go," I said to Ben and followed Larry over the edge with my single rope tied to my harness.

Larry wasted no time. He had already popped a hole in the glass and flashbanged the room, and by the time I got the barrel of my gun through the hole in the glass to cover him, I was already engulfed in flames from his quickie saw.

"We got to go," someone yelled from above just as Larry had cut the last steel bar and smashed the glass. Instead of waiting for the line that was supposed to pull the quickie saw, Larry threw the saw through the window and dove in.

With only seconds left before hitting Iranian waters, I followed immediately behind as Larry took the bridge, and I opened the door to let in the rest of the platoon, who rushed through the door like a flood of water. I'm not sure who did it, but someone got the wheel and pointed us back toward the safety of international waters.

In the face of adversity, you often have to make immediate and decisive actions—Ben getting us on the ship, Larry's diving over the edge with a single rope (not the first time he's almost gotten me killed), the platoon being stacked on the door to rush the bridge the moment it opened. It all added up and totaled out as mission success. "On time, on target," as we say. (I didn't learn this until later, but like a shark on the scent of a bleeding seal, an Iranian gunship had picked up on our activity and was closing in on our position to pounce.)

IADS

A large part of SEAL training is taken up with what we call Immediate Action Drills (IADs). They are *born in blood*—drills

ACRONYMS AND ALLITERATION

In the military, we use many acronyms so that we can convey important information quickly and accurately. Acronyms also serve as a mnemonic, or aid in memory. For example, when I was working special reconnaissance missions, we would use something called the SALUTE report to quickly observe and report on the enemy:

S = Size
A = Activity
L = Location
U = Unit
T = Time
E = Equipment

We collect and process this kind of information when, for example, we've come across any enemy presence so that the intel bubbas back in the rear can continue to build out the big picture, and the use of acronyms allows us to do so with speed and context. Similarly, in my personal life, I find myself constantly using military acronyms or ones I've created myself. For instance, if my wife and I are planning a trip, I'll constantly reference SMEAC (Situation, Mission, Execution, Admin and Logistics, Communication) to be sure I've covered all my bases. An extremely useful one when the family team is going to, for example, split up at the mall or a park is the GOTWA brief:

G = where I'm Going
O = Others I'm taking
T = Time of my return
W = What to do if I don't return

A = Actions to take if something happens (if there's an emergency while I'm gone)

Admittedly, this militant approach to a trip to Disneyland isn't always embraced by my wife, but if you ever watch us work our kids in any situation, you'll see that we cover each point of these plans in a fluid and complete manner.

stemming from mission failures that have resulted in service members being captured, injured, or killed. They are choreographed responses that we design and practice should anything go wrong at any time:

+ If we are diving and run out of air.
+ If we are skydiving and our parachute doesn't open.
+ If we are on patrol toward our objective and get contacted by the enemy, and we have to create multiple *plays* for multiple environments and directions from which an attack can come. "Contact front" (or "contact right," etc.) will be yelled if the enemy is spotted in front, and we have a drill for that.

I once spent four hours practicing what to do should someone try to attack the restaurant where we were eating while deployed deep in Africa. If you're doing the IAD, you know that somewhere at some time someone lost his life during that situation, so we take these drills very seriously. Hesitation can kill; it already had. And since SEALs operate in extremely small numbers, they depend on speed and precision. The lesson is that if we hesitate or fail to take precise actions, we die.

In the parenting world, many families have an emergency action plan or IAD for life-threatening or out-of-the-ordinary situations, such as if there's a fire in the home, if your child is approached by a stranger, or if your pregnant wife's water breaks in the middle of the night and she has to be rushed to the hospital. However, we also need them for other times of crisis. One IAD has served my family well, allowing us to deal with any and every situation as a well-informed and cohesive team.

As I discussed in chapter 1, my ex-wife, Stacey, and I have an exceptional relationship. We've remained very close since our divorce fifteen years ago and have co-parented with little to no conflict the entire time. (We, no doubt, could write a book titled *A Navy SEAL and His Ex-Wife's Guide to Divorce: When You've Lost the Battle, but Not the War.*) When we identify a behavior from Taylor or Jason that immediately needs to be stopped, started, turned up, or modified, we:

+ Rally together and talk.
+ Seek help when necessary—we all go to a family counselor at the drop of a hat.
+ Collectively choose the best strategy. It's better to execute a less-effective strategy together than to execute separate ones.
+ Execute that strategy with no hesitation.

For example, in chapter 10, we will discuss bullying and how our children need confidence in order to properly deal with conflict. Often, children can hesitate when confronted with conflict and don't stick up for themselves because they don't know what to do. Preparing and practicing IADs with your children keeps them from hesitating when they are dealing with their peers. For example, my daughter Lea has been having problems with some other girls in school who are saying things that hurt her feelings. She's afraid that if she sticks up for herself her reaction will escalate the situation and she'll end up in a fight, verbal or physical, and get in trouble with the teacher. We've been practicing her "moves" so that she can, without hesitation, react to the comments and stick up for herself in a way that she controls.

"She said I was a weakling," Lea told me.

"Lea, in a very sincere and inquisitive manner, ask your friend this question: *Did you call me that so I'd feel bad about myself?*"

Of course, I had to explain what "inquisitive" meant, and we practiced it a few times, but the next day Lea came home and told me what happened.

"She said no, that she didn't want to hurt my feelings," Lea said. "She said that she was just trying to be funny."

Lea had been empowered to do something more than just sit there and let her feelings get hurt. She could immediately react to the situation before it escalated.

ON TIME, ON TARGET

I was in Bahrain walking across the dusty parking lot of a hotel that had been converted into U.S. military barracks. My LPO (leading petty officer, like the parent of a platoon) was a guy named Mark DeCamp. One of the coolest people I've ever met, Mark was a bit older than the rest of us, but he played in a band and would travel with his guitar everywhere we went. He looked

BLUE ON BLUE

You can imagine the confusion that can ensue when a SEAL Team is conducting a dynamic operation at night. If you haven't done the work, talked about it, and come together as a team, there's a likelihood of a Blue-on-Blue situation, which is what we call it when we accidentally injure or kill someone on our own team. It's the result of a lack of communication or coordination. For many parents, this happens all the time. For example: Your son wants to go spend the night with a buddy whose parents you don't know and a couple of friends you've never heard of. One parent is concerned about the unknowns, while the other takes on the *I loved sleeping over at friends' houses when I was growing up* point of view. Both say no to the request, but the sleepover lover makes it clear that he or she doesn't agree with the decision, making the killjoy parent out to be the bad guy. (Divorced parents, in particular, often suffer from Blue-on-Blue situations that wind up *taking out* one parent, or even the children, with friendly fire.) This is why we execute IADs, why we come together and talk, so we can choose a strategy that we can both agree on when we need it most.

like a rock star as he climbed off the military transport planes. I always loved watching the reaction of the military guys working the flight line. Not only were a bunch of SEALs coming off the plane in civilian clothes, but Mark was doing it with a guitar case, which tripped them out even more.

Mark was a fairly laid-back guy, and as we walked across the parking lot he was telling me something that needed to get done. "Eric, when we get back tonight," he said, "I need you to make sure all of the trucks are cleaned out and gassed up."

Instead of replying, I just looked up at him and gave what I thought was a nod, but I guess my facial expression must have registered my displeasure at his request, because the next thing I knew his coffee cup came flying at me.

"Hey, what the fuck?" Mark said. "Remember, you're a fucking new guy. You need to fucking acknowledge me when I speak to you."

"Shit, sorry, Mark," I said. "Yeah, I got it. No problem."

Mark knew that he had high-powered go-getters to lead and that if he hesitated or failed to maintain his authority at any time, we'd end up walking all over him. When you lead a pack of alpha males and hesitate to correct them, it will not only be seen as a weakness but will create a leadership gap that will be filled in by someone or something else. Of course, he hadn't rehearsed his response as an IAD (or maybe he had), but through experience and care he developed an immediate reaction to curtail even the slightest amount of disrespect.

Chapter 4 was about *keeping up,* about being consistent in your parenting and making those rudder corrections to straighten an already forward path. However, sometimes there is a mission failure, a block in that path. You've put forth your best effort, but the odds were against you, resulting in a situation—your kid not listening, acting out, talking back. Rather than being proactive, it's a time for you, as the leader of your team, to be reactive with speed and efficiency. If someone besides Mark had chucked a coffee cup at me for not responding to his request, someone who hadn't been putting in the consistent time as our leader, I would have beat the shit out of him, or at least used some strong language, but Mark had done the work that made his instant reaction not only respected but appreciated. He had been there leading, teaching, and correcting us every step of the way. He had been keeping up, so when I questioned his authority, he needed to quickly put me back in my place. To this day, I'm conscious of how my facial expressions may or may not communicate respect.

I'm always surprised when I see a child roll his eyes or talk back to a parent, but what's more surprising is when the parent doesn't respond and correct the behavior immediately. Parents "let things go" or want to avoid "drama," or they make excuses for the behavior instead of reassessing and reacting. They hesitate and fail to correct these ineffective attitudes in the moment, and they miss the powerful learning opportunity that immediately follows the behavior. If you have been keeping up your parenting, providing the appropriate rudder corrections, you most likely have earned a place of respect and admiration, as Mark had done with his SEAL platoon. The consistency we discussed in the previous chapter has produced the space and permission to react and correct any and every slip, gap, or miss in our kids' behaviors. Therefore, when a situation arises, your reaction will elicit an expected response. A child will likely say, "Oh, sorry, Mom, I get it, no problem." If kids are used to being coached, your intense reaction is not upsetting to them but will keep them from doing it again.

COUNTING TO THREE IS NOT FOR ME

Recently, I was training Indy, my Belgian Malinois, in a grass field that was next to the back stucco walls of a row of houses, and I heard a mother yell to her child to pick up his toys and come in the house. The child clearly did not comply, because what she did next was count to ten. *Wow, I thought, that's a new record. I've heard of counting to three, but ten?* Even after having been a parent for over twenty-three years, I go nuts when I hear parents count their way toward their child's compliance. Hesitation, in this example, kills the effectiveness. All I hear is:

One . . . You don't have to listen to me the first time.
Two . . . See, I told you that you don't have to listen to me the first time.

Three . . . Oh, please let this work, so I don't have to stop what I'm doing and deal with you!

Four through Ten . . . This isn't going to work, is it? I already look like a spineless jellyfish, and now I'll have to bark out some harsh punishment that doesn't fit the original crime and look even more foolish.

Many parents like to count to three so that they can cool down and think of an appropriate reaction for whatever offense their child has committed, or so that the child can think through his compliance to the demand. For me, counting to three happens when parents haven't thought through and designed their IADs. It typically shows that someone isn't quite sure how to handle the situation. If you're one of those, just know that if we ever go camping together and I say, "Okay, everybody, get in the car," and you get stuck outside counting to three to give your kid a chance to make the right choice, I'll be leaving your ass in the woods!

DON'T BE A PRICK

When my girls act sassy or try to toss an eye roll my way or make a rude comment, my response is immediate but not harsh:

+ "Oh, no, baby, that's not how we do that. We don't roll our eyes at Momma like that. Tell me what's going on."
+ "Ella, that didn't sound like a grateful, kindhearted response. I'm sure you didn't mean it to sound that way. What is it you're trying to get done or communicate to us?"
+ "Oh, no, babe, you don't talk to your sister like that. Tell me what the problem is."

As kids learn how to problem-solve and get things done, sometimes we need to step in, react to the transgression, and work to reestablish the correct course. You don't have to be a prick when you correct your child any more than you'd have to be a prick to your car when it drifts into the other lane. Just gently move it back into its rightful place.

INTERPRETING MISBEHAVIOR

Sometimes our kids can do a shitty job of communicating their frustrations to you. Are they being disrespectful? Are their actions communicating something else? Are they mad at themselves and taking it out on you? Or are they mad at you? Have you done something?

KIDS	I WANT TO KNOW	OR DOES IT MEAN?
1) The roll of the eye	Why did you choose to do that?	Did I say or do something unfair? Did I give you some bullshit reason for saying no to something?
2) Haughty tone of voice	What are you trying to accomplish?	Have I been nagging you?
3) Ignoring me	Are you letting out frustration?	Am I trying to ask you to do something while you're busy? Right in the middle of a video game or an exciting part of a book? Did I interrupt you?
4) Having to be asked more than once to do something	Are you trying to get attention?	Am I being a lazy or distracted coach? Have I trained you to not comply until the fifth time, because that's when I always finally stop what I'm doing to help you?

TRAIN YOUR KID. LIKE A DOG.

My buddy Mike Ritland breeds Belgian Malinois for service to the SEAL Teams, and after our beloved German shepherd, Zoe,

VIOLENCE OF ACTION

SEALs can respond so quickly and so aggressively to a confrontation—whether that response is actions taken when assaulting a target or reactions to coming in contact with an enemy—that often they will appear as a much larger force. We call this *violence of action*, which keeps the enemy from getting the jump or the upper hand on us. We can't afford to let that happen to us on the battlefield any more than we can afford to let it happen on the parenting field. Late for curfew, underage drinking, drug use, inappropriate relationships, disrespectful attitudes, skipping school . . . respond quickly and aggressively to these indiscretions, and your kids won't know what hit 'em. If you're too light and inconsistent, you'll do little more than build up your kids' ability to ignore you.

died, and it came time for Belisa and me to buy another dog for protection, I thought it made sense to buy a SEAL dog from a SEAL with whom I had gone through training. Bred to capture and kill prey, a Belgian Malinois is leaner and more aggressive than a German shepherd, with a bite that crushes at 1,400 pounds per square inch. They can work in tough climates and smell drugs, explosives, or a dirt-bag human hiding in your house. Navy SEALs and other highly specialized units choose these dogs because they're small and compact, making them ideal for parachuting or climbing operations; they can even be equipped with remote video cameras that allow them to go out ahead of the human members of a team to detect danger or the presence of an enemy.

The principle of *Hesitation kills* is an important part of my training for Indy—named for my last SEAL platoon, India. Successful dog training is the application of behavior analysis science to start, stop, and modify the behaviors of a dog. At its core is operant conditioning, a term coined in 1938 by Burrhus Frederic Skinner (more commonly known as B. F. Skinner), an American psychologist and Harvard University professor. Operant conditioning is a learning process in which behavior is molded by largely controlling two factors: one's environment and the consequences related to one's behavior. Whether you're training a dog, a sniper, or a child, it is critical to understand and master the science that affects and controls behavior.

As dog trainers know, there really is no such thing as a bad dog, only bad handlers. Same goes for raising children. Are your children's bad behaviors a product of bad parenting? If so, it certainly doesn't give kids permission to act out, but it certainly can give them reason to. Think about it: Are you leading from the front? Being consistent with your parenting?

In times of trouble and conflict, our responses as parents must be swift and decisive, and our heads cool. We must have done our prep, so that our line of action has precision and effectiveness. When the situation—if your child is talking back or misbehaving, or if you're helping your child through trouble in school, such as peer pressure or bullying—is resolved and all the dust has settled, we want our children to be in a better place than they were before. We want:

+ A stronger, more focused child who understands more than ever the person you want him to be.
+ A more responsible and confident child who will never again let himself be a victim of circumstance, and will instead be a master of his behavior and universe.

+ A child who understands that even though every day we keep trying to be the person we want to be, sometimes we can be knocked out of our game, but we can meet that challenge head-on with preparation and practice.

+ A child who understands that there will be times when we as parents need to step in and correct a behavior that might harm him, your family, and your ability to live the life you want.

+ A child who knows that you love the hell out of him, and that you're making an honest effort to prevent poor choices because you want him to have the confidence to travel through adversity.

"I TOLD YOU SO"

If I have given my son advice, and he has chosen to ignore it, leading to a dangerous outcome and causing me to have to swoop in and right the wrong or reposition him back on the right track, I always make sure to tell him, "I told you so." I know this seems counterintuitive, maybe even childish, but I don't do it to rub it in. I want Jason to connect his deviance from the parenting that I have been conducting all along with the negative consequence, so that he will heed future warnings with more respect and attention as well as learn from the experience. It's a reminder that the flashing red light means not to go.

One of Sir Isaac Newton's laws of motion states that for every action in nature there is an equal and opposite reaction. A similar law holds true for parenting: For every inappropriate action committed by our children, we must take an equal and appropriate corrective action as parents.

One last thing: We've been talking so much about bad behavior in this chapter, but it's also important not to hesitate when our children exhibit good behavior. When you catch them doing the right things—saying "please" and "thank you," carrying groceries, getting homework done, waking up on time for school or work, holding the door open for little old ladies—don't hesitate to say how proud you are of them. As with dog training, positive reinforcement is a key ingredient of child-rearing. Fail to notice the good stuff, and we can extinguish those good behaviors for good.

MIKE RITLAND: TENETS OF OPERANT CONDITIONING

Mike Ritland joined the U.S. Navy at age seventeen in 1996, after being inspired by his grandfathers—both of whom had served in World War II. He graduated with BUD/S class 215 and became a member of SEAL Team 3. In April 2003, Ritland's sixteen-member SEAL Team was deployed to Iraq along with the 1st Marine Division, and they were tasked with taking the city of Tikrit. During one clearing operation, he observed a group of marines approaching a cavelike structure in a rural area outside the city. After searching thousands of buildings and similar structures without issue, they were tempted to assume that all was clear, but the platoon was alerted to danger by an explosive-detector dog. Ritland learned later that a grenade booby trap had been set in the doorway and would certainly have killed the first marines to enter. He knew instantly that he wanted to work with dogs and learn to harness their remarkable abilities to defeat the tools of modern warfare.

After twelve years of active duty as a U.S. Navy SEAL, Ritland became a BUD/S instructor and started his own company, Trikos International, to train dogs for the SEAL Teams. Today, he continues to supply working and protection dogs to a host of clients, including the Department of Homeland Security, U.S. Customs, the Border Patrol, the TSA, and the Department of Defense. He has over fifteen years of experience in importing, breeding, raising, and training multiple breeds of working dogs. He also started the Warrior Dog Foundation to help retired Special Operations dogs live long and happy lives after their service. He is the father of two girls, ages eight and ten.

I draw a lot of parallels between raising kids and training dogs. There's much similarity in terms of trying to get them to do things, to learn things, and trying to raise them up from a very young age into big, productive adults. Dogs and children, especially young children, don't understand the world the way we do, and we have to remember that. I know what *my* expectations are for a dog or for my young children; however, *they* have no idea. Therefore, working with both takes consistency and dedication, and through the principles of operant conditioning, a learning process by which learning and behavior are shaped through reinforcement and reward, we are able to build them into confident beings.

SOLID FOUNDATION

First and foremost, any relationship with a dog or a child needs to be strong and solid, with a very high level of importance. Imagine a teacher walking into an elementary school classroom and there are thirty students in there playing tag, knocking over chairs, screaming, running around, and not paying any attention to her. If she just walks up and starts calmly writing on a dry-erase board, those kids aren't going to learn anything. They're not going to absorb any of her material. She's completely wasting her time.

Conversely, if she walks in and there's a level of mutual respect there, where the kids recognize her as an authority figure, trust her, and are open to learning—they are ready to learn. Any relationship with a child, or a dog, must be rooted in that same place of trust and well-being. It can't be fear-based, whereby a teacher or parent walks into a room and the children are automatically scared to death, fearful that they're going to be physically punished. If that's the case, they're not going to learn anything either. They may sit there, quietly and respecting the rules, but they're not going to absorb much because they're going to be preoccupied with trying to avoid being punished. Same with a dog. There has to be trust and respect that comingle together.

CONTROL

You must have control of the relationship you have with your child, as with a dog. Period. Whether it's a three-year-old child who wants to mess with something that you don't want him to mess with, or a puppy that tries to chew up your shoes, they're going to test the waters on a regular basis; therefore, that level of control has to be there from you. Remember, *you* control the environmental and resource factors—i.e., food, water, going to the bathroom, free time, playtime, affection. You control when they get them and when they don't. It's a very powerful position and one that should not be taken lightly.

MOTIVATION AND POSITIVE REINFORCEMENT

In order to properly train a dog or raise a child, you need to find out what motivates that dog or child. Would training be as effective without positive reinforcement? Absolutely not. If, tomorrow, you stop getting paid for what you do for a living, how much longer are you going to do it? Exactly. Same with dogs and kids. However, as with dogs, all kids are different. For some kids, affection means a lot more than for others. For some, it's ice cream or playing catch out in the front yard or getting to play on an iPad or a video game. For dogs, it's usually pretty simple—they either like food, like attention, or like to play ball, tug, or whatever satisfies and excites their naturally inherited prey drive. You must discover what motivates them, or you'll essentially be wasting your time. For example, if a dog doesn't like to chase a ball, and I try to use a tennis ball to reward him, I'm not going to get very far in his training.

TRUST AND CONFIDENCE

Once you know what the proper motivating factors are, you can use those to build trust. With both dogs and kids, I want to be a source of all things good, but in the beginning, you need to start off neutral, even ignore them a bit. Don't flood them with rewards for no reason. Let them come to you and show you who they are, and when they do, you can start to open up a little bit and reward them with some attention. Maybe give them something to eat, play a game—whatever that particular child's motivating factors are. As with dogs, you want to show your children through body language and reinforcement that you're a good guy and trustworthy. You want to let that relationship mature and happen on its own, without forcing it. That's one of my biggest recommendations to people when they meet new dogs, and I would say the same for meeting kids, whether you're a parent, teacher, coach, or mentor—if it's the first time, don't push it, don't rush it, let the relationship happen.

With the right motivation, or positive reinforcement, you can guide your dog or your child to learn any desired activity. If your kid is scared of climbing a tree, going up a ladder, jumping into a pool, or going into his dark room at night, the answer is not to make him do it—just throw him in the water or demand that he start climbing. All that's going to do is build up a very negative context with that stimulus. You want to encourage your child to do it using positive reinforcement and rewards—smiles, words of encouragement, treats—gently coaxing him, and building his confidence so he can overcome his fear by himself.

It's a balancing act. Sometimes it takes a little bit of tough love, and sometimes it doesn't. Each circumstance and hurdle is different, which is why your training has to be very calculated and strategic in its application. When you find that you need to exercise punishment—and sometimes, as parents or dog trainers, we do—the punishment:

+ Should be the bare minimum to get the point across. It should be commensurate with the crime.
+ Should happen immediately, so that the child or the dog isn't confused about the reason for it.
+ Should be devoid of emotion. A punishment should be doled out by a calm, clear-headed dog trainer or parent.
+ Should cease once the behavior ceases. It should be water under the bridge—over and done, so you can move on.

Overall, it is important to keep your training consistent. These concepts are not easy, because they take a lot of hard work and dedication, but they are simple to understand. Building a child's confidence is probably the single most important aspect of raising a well-mannered and productive child into a successful, hardworking, decent, and confident adult. It is through successive repetition that children learn that if they apply themselves, keep trying, and never give up, they can overcome their fears and their obstacles and ultimately win.

DEBRIEF

+ In times of trouble, are your actions swift and precise because of practice, or do you panic?

+ In times of trouble, will your son's actions be swift and precise because of practice, or will he panic?

+ Do you practice IADs (Immediate Action Drills) with your family? Which ones do you have in place? Which ones do you need to put in place?

+ Do you address your kids' good and bad attitudes and behaviors in the moment, or do you hesitate? Give three examples.

+ When you're addressing an undesirable behavior, would your son describe you as kind and encouraging?

+ Does your son take your feedback to heart and look forward to future opportunities to receive corrections or input from you? Why or why not?

6

MIND OVER MATTER—IF YOU DON'T MIND, IT DOESN'T MATTER

The sky, what I could see of it, was a cold gray and seemed to leak right into the frigid Pacific Ocean as I swam steadily against the current and the wind. I was in the middle of a 5½-nautical-mile swim during the Second Phase of SEAL training. I'm not sure how long that exercise is supposed to take, but for my swim buddy and me it was a 5½-hour trek.

These swims always started a bit awkwardly for me. I never really took off smoothly. Back then, we wore pretty clunky "duck tail" wetsuit tops, the kind that had a flap hanging off the back that you pulled forward and fastened under your belly button. They were stiff and took a while to settle into. The first ten minutes of each swim was always a divided effort between stretching out the wetsuit and making progress. Besides the on-the-fly wetsuit adjustments, there were always the first few tweaks of your mask to correct any foggy areas or to tighten up any leaks. I tended to these minor but critical adjustments as I worked to get my breath in sync with my swim buddy, while he worked to identify the best landmark to use in an effort to guide the direction of our swim.

Anyone flying overhead that day or sailing nearby probably wouldn't even have noticed we were there, because we were using a combat sidestroke—an efficient, low-energy stroke that is a variation of the traditional sidestroke. The combat sidestroke has been designed and refined over multiple generations of frogmen to:

+ Enable swimmers to perform for longer periods of time without tiring.
+ Reduce swimmers' body profile in the water, which allows them to be less visible. (SEALs actually resemble a porpoise: They swim underwater, just below the surface, until they have to breathe; then their head cracks the water just enough to get some air into their lungs before they're out of sight again. Neither their arms nor their feet ever break or splash the water.)

In the ocean, there are no lap lanes to follow, and any zigzagging during a distance swim could add up to a serious amount of extra distance. Once we settled in, I'd begin to focus on the sound of my breath. As a sliver of my head broke the surface, I would inhale and draw my arm back through the water to propel myself forward. Then I would push my head back under the surface, where I'd begin a long, slow exhale while making a slight hum in the back of my throat. Once the rhythm was set, the sounds of my breath and the bubbles from my exhale would become hypnotic, and my sense of space and time would begin to drift.

Five and a half hours is a long time to be in the water. I'd start off with my mask fairly tight on my face, but once the headaches set in, I'd have to loosen it a bit. This would periodically allow saltwater in the mask, which I wouldn't notice until my nose blasted it up into my eyes in a stinging spray. My lips and the tip of my tongue eventually began to shrivel up and prune as if they were getting pickled by the sea. Since I preferred to swim on one side of my body the entire time, the bile and saltwater that made their way into my stomach would settle and then produce burning nausea on the occasions when I'd have to roll over to see where we were or to stretch out any cramps. Every thirty minutes or so, I'd make a point of checking my testicles to make sure they hadn't, yet again, tucked themselves back into my pelvis in an act of either self-preservation or protest.

Although each and every bit of physical discomfort could produce a bit of misery and add to the challenge, they paled in comparison to the mental discomforts that would ensue. I don't even remember my swim buddy being there. I knew he *was* there, somewhere, but it's not like we talked to one another or anything. We were both completely in our heads and focusing on the task at hand.

Mental self-discipline and willpower are critical to SEAL student success and can help you overcome many physical obstacles and challenges. That day in the ocean, I used all kinds of mental strategies, particularly visualization, to get me through that swim:

+ I thought about past successes, including images of myself at thirteen years old in my tae kwon do uniform. I'd replay the moment I sat against the wall waiting my turn to spar.

+ I thought about what I was doing right now and how it would bring me closer to where I wanted to be. I could see myself in the water—an out-of-body experience of sorts—and I remember thinking, *That's what a Navy SEAL looks like before graduation.*

✦ I thought about the future accomplishments and experiences that this swim would lead to. I fantasized about all the secret missions I'd perhaps be on someday, how everything I was doing could lead to becoming a law enforcement officer or an FBI agent or just something more than what I was before I entered the water. I thought about how great it would feel the next time I took Taylor or Jason to the ocean to swim and told them how long and how far Dad swam, and how much better a waterman Dad had become. I could see the through-line of my life from under the surface of the water, how the person I was now would morph into the person I was to become in just a few hours.

Inhale, exhale, keep swimming.

I would have conjured up and thought about anything that would have gotten me through that swim, and as I neared what I thought was the end of the exercise, my mental mettle was put to the test.

Just a few miles south of Coronado, California, where we began our swim, there's a small, nearly abandoned base that at the time was called the NRRF (Naval Radio Receiving Facility). The NRRF was home to a mysterious, and very large, circular structure called a Wullenweber antenna with a 1,300-foot diameter and a height of over 100 feet. It was referred to as the Elephant Cage.

The Elephant Cage was a leftover listening antenna used for electronic espionage. Its circular design surrounded a building full of radio equipment and operators whose full-time job was to listen for signals coming from anywhere and everywhere. During the Cold War, Elephant Cages were planted around the world so that enemy signals could be triangulated and used to target their source's precise location. On this particular day, the Elephant Cage seemed to both triangulate and hold my swim buddy and me indefinitely in the precise location of *not yet there.*

Because of the Elephant Cage's size, it felt like you were close to it the moment you had it in your sights. And because it's located close to the finish of the swim, it gave you the feeling that you were almost there. We were not allowed to wear watches, so we'd eventually lose all concept of time as we entered the homestretch of the swim. The Elephant Cage never seemed to get closer— stroke after stroke, almost as if we were treading water. It was like trying to swim past the moon.

That's the kind of thing that can get in your head and manipulate your thoughts. At one point, my swim buddy and I decided we'd just sprint for it. We swam hard for what must have been thirty minutes before we allowed ourselves to look back up at it. Sure enough, it was still there—no closer, no farther—as if we were caught in an aquatic tracker beam.

People who know me would assume that because I like to swim and surf, a swim like this would be easy for me, but there's a very big difference between liking the water and swimming in it for 5½ nautical miles. On this day, it would not be my passion for the water nor my love of the ocean that would get me through. Those things faded away sometime after the second hour. It would only be the thoughts in my head that would win the day and counteract the elements that were physically taking a toll on my body. As a SEAL, you get to do some pretty amazing things that, on their own, for short periods of time, would be considered fun—parachuting, shooting, hiking, climbing, diving, swimming, and even boating on the ocean. However, once they become your profession, the things you do all day every day, they become as hard and demanding as any other job.

> "People think that when SEALs go on a mission they're just these superheroes who somehow magically are successful in the things they do when, in fact, it all comes down to planning ahead. We know exactly what's going to happen before it happens. I extend that principle to my daily living. Most people wake up each day, and they just let the day happen. They have no purpose for the day in general. People talk about the importance of goal setting, but they don't get out of bed each morning and say, 'Okay, today, I'm going to do this. I'm going to have a good day. I'm going to get this, this, and this done.' Something like that is so easy to do, but nobody does it. That's why I teach my boys to think about their days as if they were missions. What is the objective? What do you want to achieve? It makes them not only more productive but also more appreciative of their time."
>
> **—CHRIS SAJNOG, RETIRED NAVY SEAL**

Similarly, even though I've wanted to be a father ever since I can remember, fatherhood, once it was a full-time gig, became a demanding job that I don't always love. For example, as a father I don't get to:

+ Surf whenever I want, as long as I want. Everyone gets cold and eventually wants to go home.
+ Watch what I want to watch on TV. I'm not sure if we even get any channels besides the Disney Channel.
+ Travel without restrictions or safety concerns. Kids don't have great situational awareness and are terrible at spotting threats.
+ Have a conversation without being interrupted. It's like my mic is turned off or they can't see the phone up to my ear while I'm talking.

+ Hike the Pacific Crest Trail from Mexico to Canada for six months. Child Protective Services doesn't allow you to leave kids home alone for that long. I looked it up.

+ Camp outside for days on end without having to worry about bathrooms. I guess crapping in the woods is a skill that needs to be developed over time.

+ Have personal belongings. I'm pretty sure my kids must conspire to hide my gear from me. There's just no way they can be this consistent without intentionally trying.

+ Spend an entire day or two biking, climbing, hiking, surfing, or doing anything that I love to do without having to stop for lunch or bathroom breaks, slow down, or cut out early to do homework. Their life often gets in my way.

+ Have a house without "stuff" everywhere. I keep my gear squared away and ready to go at all times. These people don't seem to understand the concept of being ready at a moment's notice. It takes them twenty minutes to get out the door—maybe eighteen, if there was a fire.

I submit this short (yes, there's more) list because I, like many other fellas out there, feel guilty about some of the aspects of being a father that I don't love. And in the twenty-three years I've been a father, I've used the same process to endure the less than exciting and potentially tedious parts of fatherhood that I used during that 5½-nautical-mile swim:

+ I think about how much I love my kids. Love is a choice, and I make that choice every day.

✦ I think about how happy whatever I'm doing makes my kids. When I turn my focus to their happiness, rather than my own, all activities become rewarding.

✦ I think about what a great father I am striving to be and how much better I can be tomorrow. With any skill, we get better over time. Consistent effort eventually leads to effortless execution (which we will discuss in chapter 8).

✦ I think about how and where I am leading my family. This life goes beyond me. I'm creating a legacy that will go beyond them.

✦ I think about how every stage is temporary and will be gone before I know it. With two adult kids, I can tell you that your time together goes by fast. I try to remember all of the "last times"—they fall asleep on my chest or my face, take up the whole bed, or reach out to hold my hand. These all will eventually have a last time, and I know I will miss them desperately.

✦ I remind myself that I am setting an example for my kids on how to live their life. I'm setting the standards for how they should be as a father, friend, and spouse. I'm teaching them what they should expect from the people around them now and in the future.

✦ Once I became a father, my job, my world, became *we before me,* and that has carried my mind over all matter.

We don't always realize we are practicing mental toughness. Every day, we probably have something we don't want to do—clean the garage, mow the lawn, pay bills—and we push ourselves to do it. Being a parent requires mind over matter on a daily basis.

Inhale, exhale, keep swimming.

NOT GOOD, NOT BAD

Often, when we think of the concept of mind over matter, we think of it in terms of having either a good or bad attitude:

+ A *good* attitude would mean that you wouldn't let a cold, tired, or frustrating situation stop you from reaching your objective.
+ A *bad* attitude would mean that you succumbed to discomfort, boredom, or insufficient motivation and failed to perform the evolution.

However, what if instead of thinking about a situation as good or bad, you instead redefine that situation as a building block, which transcends mere attitude? In other words, imagine if that very activity that you dread was going to make you a better father, help you learn a new skill, or take you further in your career. Like lifting a weight or running an extra mile. Something that makes you stronger needn't be something you must dread or just endure.

TURNING A NEGATIVE INTO A POSITIVE

Mental toughness and whatever you use to power through an activity—grit, perseverance, and passion—play a significant role in a successful life. They are developed in increments and small, consistent wins, and they have the power to change a negative experience into a positive one. How we experience our surroundings and situations is more a matter of choice than we realize.

Our bodies merely perceive input (matter), but it is our minds that produce the meaning.

I was about three weeks into the First Phase of SEAL training when my alarm started blaring at 4:00 A.M. I remember feeling this incredible despair. I could barely lift my eyelids. I don't think I had ever felt that tired in my life. There was a constant ringing in my head, my legs felt as if someone had hit them repeatedly with a rubber mallet throughout the night, the calluses on my hands had peeled off, leaving bloody holes, and I could barely walk. The SEAL instructors had done a number on me and had beaten up my body badly the day before—sprints into the ocean, endless squats, push-ups, pull-ups, dips, crunches, verbal harassment late into the night—with only a few hours of sleep to recover.

The next morning, I found myself buckled over in a quasi-push-up position, my body covered with sand—on my face, in my ears, between my thighs, in my mouth. Both my quadriceps seized up because of muscle cramps, and I could taste the trickle of blood as it made its way from my nose through the sand and onto my lips. I was in bad shape. It was one of the few times in training I could feel my mood slipping.

Suddenly, I had a thought that immediately changed the way I felt, that made me forget about the bruises and the exhaustion. I even let out a small chuckle. I realized that the SEAL instructors who were training me hadn't actually done anything to me. They hadn't laid a single hand on me, or forced me to do any of those sprints and lunges. They hadn't stopped me from going to bed. They hadn't forced me out of bed for a timed 4-mile run in the soft sand. All they did was tell me what they wanted me to do in order for me to become a SEAL. I had done all those things to myself and, more importantly, by myself. From that day on, in the two years it takes to become qualified as an operational SEAL, I continued to push myself well beyond my perceived limits, getting stronger both physically and mentally. The SEAL instructors had become like a set of braces for me, allowing me to build my mind over matter strength.

After having been a SEAL instructor for a number of years, I developed a much deeper knowledge about what it takes for someone to make it through what has become known as the most difficult training in the world. Since 2008, I've been repurposing that knowledge for high-performing individuals and businesses, and I have found that in both cases, those who "make it" share this in common: not just the ability to endure pain, but the ability to not even feel it. SEAL training or success isn't just about enduring the misery. SEAL training is about turning the perception of misery off or even turning it into something pleasurable. Many SEALs got so good at doing this that we found ourselves actually enjoying things like Surf Torture (see chapter 9) and running indefinitely.

Where does this frame of mind come from? It comes from believing in a higher purpose, focusing on our objective, and having a level of passion for something beyond reason.

ON HIGHER GROUND

We must learn to become solely responsible for what's going on inside us. I'm not just talking about the obvious stuff, like not letting others upset you or being too shy to speak in front of a group of people. I'm talking about the stuff that is *deep* inside of you—the very things that seem hardwired, unchangeable, and part of our DNA. The things that seem to make us who we are. But even

TREATING OTHERS

About three years before I became a SEAL, I had my first experience with Special Operations as a Recon Corpsmen while serving with the marines. It was my job to monitor and care for the health of all the team members. One day, there was a battalion-wide "Hump"—a long hike with lots of weight in your pack—that included not just my Recon platoon, but all of the administrative marines, male and female, from the entire battalion as well. There had to be close to a thousand people hiking, sweating, and carrying more weight than they were conditioned for. It was hot and people were dropping like flies. I spent four hours running up and down this extremely long line of people administering first aid and giving IVs to those who became dangerously, or at least looked, dehydrated. By the time I treated a patient and helped him or her into the ambulance that trailed behind us, I'd have to run all the way back to the front to help someone else. Some of the people I helped had given up well before their body had, and others had pushed themselves to their physical limits.

It was an amazing time in my life, because I began to realize the power that would form inside of me when I focused on what was outside of me. As I ran the lines of people over and over, I really learned that some of the greatest mental strength came from helping others. Not once did I notice any of the four blisters I had developed, nor the three-inch gash that had formed on my back from my heavy and awkward medical equipment. All I thought about was finding the next person falling out of ranks and how I could save that person. Altruism for me became the most pure and potent form of mind over matter.

these can be overcome when you focus on a mission or a higher purpose.

For example, one of my deepest personality traits is a seemingly hardwired fear of picking up women, and a large part of intelligence work is about gaining assets—creating relationships everywhere you go so that you can potentially leverage them for current or future missions. I was training in Virginia Beach, and it was my mission to develop relationships with people who worked by the harbor. The training was intense and high budget, and it was a regular occurrence for the government to hire actors and actresses to engage with us and test our ability to quickly build rapport and win them over.

Near the final phase of my training, I was at a favorite restaurant of mine that I liked to visit in order to plan out my routes and think through my day. It was a cold and foggy day, and I had gotten there right at the busiest time of day. A mildly attractive waitress whom I had not yet seen before approached me to take my order. She spoke with a thick Russian accent and seemed a bit flirtatious. Without thought or care, I chatted her up within earshot of about five other diners, and within minutes I had asked her to go out that night. Now, I know this may not seem like a big deal, but for me it is *huge*—something that I would normally hate and never do, especially when multiple people are listening in. The waitress agreed, gave me her phone number, and the date was set.

Later that night, I was talking with one of the instructors and told him about the asset I had potentially gained. I guess I was assuming that she was one of the paid actresses, since I hadn't seen her before that day.

"Dude," my instructor said, leaning in with an odd amount of interest. "She's not one of ours."

"What do you mean?" I asked, confused.

"I mean, you got a hot Russian chick to go out with tonight. Have fun."

"What?! You're fucking kidding me!" I replied incredulously. Here I was years into my second marriage, and now I get good at picking up chicks? What a waste.

Not knowing what to do, I promptly picked up my government-issued mobile phone and called Belisa. "Babe, I accidently picked up a Russian waitress."

How? There wasn't a moment I hesitated or felt nervous or embarrassed, because my purpose was so high—mission success—and anything and everything that would, could, or used to bother me or make me uncomfortable was gone. A seemingly "hard-wired" part of my personality—shyness—had been easily overcome by my mind.

> *"When Eric told me about the Russian waitress, my response was, 'Well, what are you going to do now?' Neither one of us recalls what happened next, if he called her back or waved her off, but Eric was very proud of himself for managing to ask someone out and having her say yes. I like to tell him the incident is yet another example of why he is lucky to be married to me when most women would have flipped out on him."*
>
> **—BELISA DAVIS**

PRODUCING PASSION

Mind over matter is not always a simultaneous experience, an exercise we mentally perform to counter and overcome a physical hardship. Sometimes the work is done ahead of time—a form of conditioning that happens even when we don't realize it.

It was a particularly crisp morning, just before sunrise, and my SEAL class was standing before the Pacific Ocean. You knew the water was cold, because it looked like it was—a murky, dark, and impenetrable gray. Instructor Samuels informed us we'd be waiting for a while, because the safety boats were running late, and I was standing there for about forty-five minutes feeling content and looking out to the horizon when the guy next to me suddenly snapped.

"I can't take this anymore!" he said.

"Take what?" I asked, a bit startled, having been snapped out of my daydream.

"The fucking cold water. This is bullshit."

"What cold water?" I asked. We weren't standing in the cold water yet, and the boats weren't even on their way. We were just standing on the beach.

"Dude, the water we're about to get into!" he said before turning and walking over to the instructor. I never saw the guy again.

Two men standing on the same beach. With the same gear. At the exact same time. One was suffering, and the other was having the time of his life. Why?

My friend Chris Campbell was standing on the other side of the dude, and when the guy left, Chris came closer and said, "Hell, we'd be doing this anyways if we weren't here."

"What do you mean?" I asked him.

"We'd be hitting dawn patrol right about now," said Chris, a fellow surfer.

He was right. The ability to continuously enter the cold water was a behavior both Chris and I had associated with our love of surfing and was developed over the years to become a positive experience for us. The hard mental work, in a sense, had already been done in tiny positive increments over the years.

"Times of inactivity are a critical aspect of child development. Quiet moments inspire introspection and creativity. They are times when children can just be in their own space without worrying about external influences. My wife and I have quiet time for our girls when they go into their rooms, we shut the door, and they have to find something to do for a half hour to forty minutes. They have very distinct play areas where they have arts and crafts, books, and toys, and they have to go there and create and explore. We also have outside quiet time on a regular basis. We live a couple of miles from the beach, so we spend a lot of time there, and the beach is the greatest place on the planet to be inventive, because I can bring my girls down there with a shovel, dig a big hole, and just let them go. You can see that creativity pour out of them.

"This need for quiet time was a valuable lesson that I learned from my parents. My dad is an incredibly artistic, creative guy. He's a lawyer, so he's very cerebral, too, and one of the first things that my brother and I learned as kids was how to draw. We would spend hours drawing together and create worlds and characters, and this became the ignition point for our creativity in our lives. I think when you fuel that creativity with children, you're setting them up for self-awareness, for personal growth, and for the ability to be in those quiet moments and be okay and comfortable with themselves."

—DAVID RUTHERFORD, FORMER NAVY SEAL

I'm working with a young man named Brent who wants to be a SEAL, and his preparation for SEAL training started long before he ever dove into the ocean or laced up his running shoes. It started years ago when he was just daydreaming about it. For a lot of SEALs, the idea of becoming a SEAL nags you and haunts your thoughts for a very long time. I've heard it called *having the song in you*. It's something you gotta do, your *passion*. When I was young and became aware of the SEAL Teams, I didn't have all of the passion that I'd require to make it through training. Passion, for me, was and has always been a bit of a process. I had spent over six years in the navy before I graduated from SEAL training. During that time, my passion for being a SEAL ebbed and flowed like a coastal tide, and I got sidetracked more than once. I remember once somebody even said to me, "If you were going to be a SEAL you'd have already done it by now." From the time that guy said that to me, I went to BUD/S, quit, got out of the navy for a year, moved to another state, entered the Navy Reserves, got another contract to go back to BUD/S, moved my wife and two kids back to California, and graduated.

Plenty of stuff (matter) gets in the way of our dreams and goals, and the same will happen to our sons. It's important to remember that life is a long game and just because the fire flickers and sputters doesn't mean it's not going to burn even brighter in the future. Our passions are no more fixed than our preferences.

It was that daydream and that desire that got Brent to start training the first time. A lot of people, including himself, didn't think he was committed to it enough, and his first run at it kind of fizzled, but the pilot light remained.

I can remember training together in the beginning. I was pretty happy with my forty-year-old self, because I was able to quickly punish him during any kind of workout and especially on

SWAGGER

My buddy Larry Yatch and I were getting a couple of hot dogs at Costco. As we were walking back from the ketchup stand, Belisa said, "Man, you boys stand out so much."

"What do you mean?" I asked, ever-sensitive about looking like we were in the military.

"Like our haircuts or the way we dress?" Larry asked with concern.

"No, you guys look so confident. You have a swagger that separates you from all of the other people around you."

For years, I thought this confident sort of swagger that SEALs are known for had to do with all of the training we went through (which, no doubt is a contributing factor). However, as I've gotten older, I've come to believe that this swagger comes from experience, knowing what we should concern ourselves with and what we shouldn't.

When you're deployed around the world and are briefed on and have seen firsthand the planet at its worst, you tend to not concern yourself with the little things that most people seem to fret and spin on—neighborhood gossip, Facebook chatter, designer labels, baby bumps, wardrobe malfunctions, or anything any celebrity has to say about anything. We don't even listen to that stuff. When your mind is on the matters of the world, when you're thinking about people dying or getting sold into slavery, you tend to not give a fuck about whether the Starbucks barista spells your name wrong on your coffee cup. Giving our sons a higher sense of purpose, big and worthy problems to solve, not only allows them to overcome peer pressure and persevere through times of awkwardness or discomfort, but also produces the sort of confidence that will allow them to rise above and walk through all of the sheep shit that would normally slow them down.

long runs. I'd taunt him toward the end of grueling runs by telling him that if he could beat me up the final hill we'd stop, but if I won we'd do the entire run over again. Even though I knew this kid personally, I couldn't go easy on him. Any false hope or sense of security would only hurt him in the long run. SEAL training is not a support group. It's only for those who can help themselves. It didn't take me long to run his current desire to become a SEAL right out of him, but I wasn't worried about breaking his spirit because I knew that if the song was in him there'd be nothing I could do to snuff it out. His flame only needed to burn a bit hotter.

A little over a year later, he was back with a vengeance. I fully expected to be able to smoke him again, but this time the harder I tried the stronger he got. Any ideas I had of trying to push him past his limits quickly faded. It didn't take but a few weeks before I told him, "Buddy, we're going to have to do separate workouts. I can coach you during yours, but I can no longer keep up with you. I'll only slow you down."

THE EDGE SHOT

I believe each of our minds can overcome any and every situation, do the right thing in the face of peer pressure, make the right choice rather than the easy one, and even disregard all levels of pain—but for how long?

When I was on that 5½-nautical-mile swim, I'd inhale, exhale, and fall into the trance required to carry me through the over five hours of swimming. Once I was in the zone, time and space would seemingly stand still. It was when pain, discomfort, or distraction pulled me out of my hyper state of performance that I'd struggle to overcome the matter at hand. For me, the foundation of mental management and toughness has always been in direct proportion to my ability to remain focused.

Brandon Webb and I spent a considerable amount of time mastering our skills as sniper instructors, which included our ability to mentally engage and, on occasion, unravel any vulnerable or underdeveloped mindsets. We were just about halfway through the six-week shooting portion of sniper school on a large range in Coalinga, a small town in central California. About 75 miles south of Soledad, the setting for Steinbeck's *Of Mice and Men,* Coalinga sits cornered between long-stretching coastal foothills and the scattered pumps of the big oil company that owned every bit of the matted land surrounding the range. Dry, hot, and dusty describes not only the environment, but the moods of those who'd already spent three long weeks training over twelve hours a day.

"Team Three, did you miss your target?"

"Team Eight, are you looking in the right direction?"

Brandon and I were conducting what we called an "Edge Shot"—a training scenario designed to pressure-test a sniper's ability to maintain his focus for long and undetermined amounts of time. We made it a practice to mix in our commentary in an effort to verbally break their focus.

"Hey, Team Three, did your target just pop up?" Brandon randomly said.

The shooter came off his gun to look over his shoulder and reply, "No, nothing has come up. I've been on my scope the entire time." Just as he turned to get back on his gun, the radio crackled: *Team Three. Miss.*

Both the shooter and his spotter heard it and spun around in protest. "What the fuck? We were talking to you when the target came up!"

"Sorry, bro. You missed it. You gotta stay on your gun, homie," I said casually.

"Why in the hell were you guys talking to us when we're trying to take a fucking test here?"

"Dude, calm down. That was the test," Brandon snapped back with a bit of an edge to his voice.

"That's bullshit, man," the shooter snapped. "We're supposed to be testing right here and you guys are fucking with us. It's a shooting test. Now we failed because we looked back at you?"

"Yes, you're being tested right now, dude. This is about your ability to focus, maintain your composure, and hit the target. You're failing right now as you keep talking," Brandon said as he whispered into the radio, "Raise Team Three's target." He turned his radio up as loud as it would go and walked closer to the disgruntled shooting pair that was now just sitting there staring at each other. Once again the radio crackled: "Team Three. Miss again."

"Missed again, dude. Better luck next time," I said as we walked away.

The ability to put your mind over matter, manage it, and build it up is something that all of us struggle with. It requires focus; the deeper the focus, the more potent its power. Our busy, jammed-packed lives—plus the constant interruption of phone calls, text messages, and other virtual notifications—pull us out of our flow and toss us into the strong currents of our life's swim.

Our minds can't be used as the powerful tools that they are if they're taken out of the game and sidelined. Fathers must stay on their guns and learn the mental toughness they need to never take their eyes off their target, and teach their sons to do the same. You can do it, and so can they.

Inhale, exhale, and keep swimming.

KIMS

As a sniper or intelligence operative doing recon and surveillance, stopping to take notes can either get you caught or killed. You're either so heads down crawling on your belly or you're in a non-permissive environment where the presence of notes, digital or on paper, can get you arrested for espionage. Therefore, you have to rely on your mental acumen.

In Rudyard Kipling's 1901 novel, *Kim,* the hero, named Kim, plays what is now commonly known as KIMS games during his training as a spy. These games are used in sniper and intelligence training to sharpen an operator's ability to observe and remember target details.

To capture the trust, admiration, and respect of the snipers I taught, I dove excessively into high-level performance strategies—exaggerating the example—such as teaching myself how to memorize a deck of cards in order. I got so good at memorizing stuff that I could read a thirty-plus person list of my students once and memorize all of their phone numbers. When I would demonstrate this to them, they knew I had something exceptional to offer. I got to where I could walk around an entire city block and— without taking notes or making a video or audio recording—

remember the details, from addresses to how many doors there were or how far apart they were. It's been another handy trick from the SEAL Teams that I'll occasionally break out while teaching my kids spelling or the like.

Ironically, if you ask my wife, she'll tell you that I don't remember a damn thing, and it's true. This ability to memorize large chunks of data is just another example of what we can do when we put our minds to it. Our minds are extremely powerful. We need only learn how to tap into them.

LARRY YATCH: SELF-REGULATION

There's a part of the brain called the anterior cingulated cortex (ACC) that controls self-regulation, your body's ability to regulate on three levels—physical, mental, and emotional. With regard to SEAL Training, most people focus on physical self-regulation as the key to success, and that's obvious, right? The instructors are going to put you in cold water and make you stay there even though your body is telling you to get out. They're going to make you do push-ups until you can't do push-ups anymore. They're going to make you run longer than you think you can, and you're going to stay up later than you want to stay up. Self-regulation is your mind's ability to continue doing that physical exercise regardless of your body's desire to stop. The people who don't have the ability to physically regulate quit early on in training.

What isn't quite as obvious is that there is significant emotional self-regulation that is being conducted on a daily basis as well. Instructors are always telling you that you're no good, that you're not going to finish, that it's impossible for you to finish. They're going to make fun of you. They're going to try and make you upset. They're going to try and make you sad. They do this because they know if someone becomes upset, sad, and frustrated, he is going to have a harder time self-regulating and will eventually quit. We see a lot of SEAL students quit not because they physically can't get through the training, but because they can't take the emotional abuse. However, the abuse isn't personal. The SEAL instructors don't honestly think you're no good. They just want to test you and push you, because, one day, when you are at war or in a military conflict, there's going to be significant need to be able to regulate emotionally.

The third level of self-regulation is mental. The instructors are going to put you in situations where you can't win. They're going to force you to continuously try to solve problems that appear to be unsolvable—and sometimes they are. A typical example: The SEAL instructors might tell you the next evolution will take place at the swimming pool and that they want you there in ten minutes. The swimming pool is a mile and a half away. And you know from experience that it probably takes about twenty minutes to get there, not ten. You could make it there in ten minutes as a class, if you really hustle, but you'd lose a quarter of your classmates, because some will not be able to keep up. There are two possible results: 1) Run fast, show up on time with three-quarters of the class, and get in trouble, or 2) Show up as a class, all of you late, and get into trouble. In that example, the instructors are:

+ Testing physical regulation, because you've got to run to the pool, you've got to run as fast as you can, and you're going to have people who can't run that fast.

✦ Testing mental self-regulation—how you solve that problem, which doesn't appear to be solvable.

✦ Testing emotional self-regulation, because when you show up, no matter what you did, you're already wrong.

When you combine all three levels, what the instructors are *really* testing you on is how well you perform, the choices you make, given the parameters you have. SEAL instructors know that the ACC controls all three types of self-regulation, and they also know that if one type is drained the others suffer as well. We have all experienced being physically exhausted (physical self-regulation) and having a hard time keeping our tempers (emotional self-regulation) and making good decisions (mental self-regulation). The decline of one type of regulation weakens the others. Similarly, we can *strengthen* the whole system—essentially, "hack" the neuroscience—by having a strong, clear purpose that gives us direction and passion, and can pass the benefits of our work from one regulation type to another. That means that if we physically push ourselves, we will be better able to control our emotions or focus mentally, and if we work hard to regulate mentally—for example, by studying or meditating—we will be better able to perform physically.

As a parent, it is important to remember that your children's eventual success in any field will be dependent on their ability to self-regulate in one, if not all three, of the domains. Therefore, you must continuously build an environment in which they can struggle (regulate) and learn that the struggle is as beneficial as reaching the objective. When it comes to being successful, those of us—parents, children, Navy SEALs, CEOs—who have a great ability to self-regulate physically, emotionally, and mentally tend to be the most successful.

DEBRIEF

+ What does mental toughness mean to you?
+ What is something your son has failed at because he couldn't endure the pain or discomfort that came from it?
+ What is something that you've succeeded at despite the overwhelming discomfort?
+ How do you build up your son's mental toughness?
+ Create a list of things you dislike to do as a father.
+ Now explain how both you and your son benefit by you doing those things.
+ What are some ways you've turned negative or bad situations into positive and pleasurable ones?
+ How does shifting your focus outward to others help you better enjoy life? How does this connect to creating passion in your life? How can you teach your son this?
+ Are you good at self-regulating? How can you get better at it? Have you taught your son this skill?

7

IT PAYS TO BE A WINNER

I was sprinting past the Slide for Life on the west side of the O Course just a hundred yards from the ocean on the fourth conditioning run of First Phase. We had been running in the soft sand for about an hour when the instructor leading the run unexpectedly picked up the pace just before he returned to the back gate of the compound.

As the class began to spread out like the tail of a sputtering comet, I found myself with a large group of SEAL students. I decided to stick with them, thinking there would be safety in numbers, so I had my head down and was concentrating on landing my feet in the divots of impacted sand left behind by the feet of the guy in front of me.

"Hurrrrrry up, hurrrrrry up, you fellas had better catch up!" echoed the BUD/S instructor's voice over the PA (Public Announcement) system of the white 4 x 4 van that trailed behind us, one of the baddest-assed ambulances I'd ever seen.

I turned my head to get a glimpse of the poor fools falling

behind and was startled by what I saw: the grill of the van. *I* was the poor fool the instructor was talking to!

I quickly ran off to the side of the group and discovered that we were a good 50 yards behind the rest of the class. I took off at a sprint. In the distance, I spotted the instructor standing at the finish line. His arm was going up and down, and just before I got to him, he chopped it down and left it there.

"Oh, so close," he said to me and the group of guys near me. "Hit the surf."

As I crested the sand berm on the way back from hitting the surf, soaking and out of breath, I could see the fellas who had finished the evolution on time; they were stretching and drinking from Gatorade bottles wrapped with white medical tape and stenciled with their last names. That had almost been me.

"Line up and get ready to race," the arm-chopping instructor said while pointing toward an imaginary starting line in the soft sand. "First three across the line are secured." He raised his hand to start the race as we got into position. This was the Goon Squad, as discussed in chapter 5, and in order to join the others for some much needed rest and hydration, I'd have to beat out the other guys who were stuck with me. I'd have to win.

"Ready," the instructor said, "go!"

Amped up with anticipation, as this was my first race in BUD/S, I took off with everything I had. For the entire sprint, I vacillated between the idea of putting out and the idea of conserving my energy for the next run: If I went all out and didn't get secured, I'd be in for a world of hurt, but if I went for it and won, all of the effort would be worth it. To this day, I'm incredibly thankful that as I closed in on the guy in front of me I chose to go for it, because I was the third to cross the finish line, while he was the first of the losers whose suffering continued for a good hour after that.

Being a SEAL is all about winning, and throughout training the instructors take every opportunity to point out the benefit of passing a test or beating an opponent. They'll say, "It pays to be a winner," and reward those who win, while hammering the shit out of those who lose. But what does it really mean to win? Is it really only about crossing a finish line before someone else? Is it only about coming in first?

In BUD/S, we did a lot of racing and head-to-head competitions, for sure, but their ultimate purpose wasn't to see who could run, climb, or swim the fastest. The instructors taught us that winning and beating someone are two very different things. When we beat someone, it's over. Maybe we'll get a medal for it; maybe we won't. Winning, on the other hand, is when we gain a skill, grow as an athlete, and become better, stronger, and more confident. And that has no end.

SEAL training and life are long games. The level of performance you must reach to succeed at both will be greater than that which can be accomplished simply by beating someone in a single race or evolution. Often, star athletes or college football players struggle in BUD/S, because success for them had always come from being better than the next guy. In SEAL training, success comes from becoming better than the guy you were yesterday.

"My dad is engaged with everything I do, and is very competitive. For example, if I claim I can do more pull-ups than he can, the competition starts, and if I do twenty, he'll only do twenty-one, not because he can't do more, but just to get under my skin a bit. Another time, the two of us were finishing up a 5-mile run, and he said to me, 'We can turn

> *around right now, or we can race up the last hill, and if*
> *you win, we're done, but if you lose, we have to turn around*
> *and run back.' I knew my chances were slim, but I had no*
> *option but to start sprinting and to hope he might trip on*
> *his shoelace or something merciful like that."*
>
> **—JASON DAVIS**

A WINNING MINDSET

As a father, my role is to teach my kids the difference between beating someone and winning. It's my role to guide them and help them understand that as long as they keep getting better, faster, and stronger, they're going to succeed. How do you know if you're winning as a dad? In footraces and sports, winning is pretty straightforward. You're either first or you're not. If you're not fast enough or strong enough, if you don't cross the finish line first, you train until you do or realize that you cannot. In day-to-day life, there aren't people to your left or right to beat. Winning isn't so obvious, but it is achieved every day by:

+ Helping your son to develop a skill, such as climbing or long division.
+ Helping him to achieve a goal, whether it's getting into his first-choice college or working up the courage to ask out a hot girl.
+ Helping him to overcome hurdles stemming from the internet, TV, alcohol, and whatever keeps him from being active, creative, and focused.
+ Helping him to keep his promises and commitments to be somewhere when he said he would.

✦ Putting workout time on your calendar and then honoring that time by actually working out.

Each of these are tiny victories that pay off a little bit each day and then, all of them together, can pay off big in life. The secret to passing BUD/S is the same secret to being a man or a father or a successful individual: If you always try your best and don't quit, you will eventually win.

PUPPY BELLY

In BUD/S, many people quit just after a meal. Why? Because when they eat they sit down, settle in, and get comfortable; they get *puppy belly*—that warm, post-Thanksgiving meal, cuddly nap feeling. They feel satiated, and the last thing they want to do is to make a sugar cookie or hit the surf. A body that is in motion tends to stay in motion, and one that is not . . . well, you know how that goes.

PARTICIPATION AWARDS ARE FOR BATTLES WON, NOT THE WAR

The first win of any activity or training is simply to show up. I don't know if there is any other organization that rewards people for showing up as much as the military. Here is a quick list of some of the military awards I received as a member of my team:

Joint Service Medal: For playing a critical role in the preparation and maintenance of mission-essential gear and ensuring that all equipment was in superior condition and ready for use at a moment's notice; and for an attention to detail, dedication to operation success, and technical knowledge and leadership during the planning and execution phases of a sensitive mission.

Navy/Marine Corps Achievement Medal: For professional achievement while serving as advanced sniper instructor at Naval Special Warfare Group One Training, and displaying exceptional technical knowledge and organizational skill, which played a pivotal role in the development and implementation of the new Naval Special Warfare sniper course.

Navy/Marine Corps Achievement Medal: For professional achievement while serving as a lead sniper for SEAL Team 3 India Platoon, and for professionalism that was reflected in the countless hours spent with various helicopter squadrons developing standard operating procedures for combat operations.

Joint Service Achievement Medal: For meritorious achievement as Mission Tracker, Combined Joint Special Operations Task Force-South, Special Operations Command Central, Khandahar, Afghanistan, in support of Operation Enduring Freedom.

Certificate of Commendation: For superior performance of duty while serving at Headquarters Battalion, 1st Marine Division, and for performing duties in an exemplary and highly professional manner, including superior triage management and emergency trauma skills.

"There are a couple words you will never hear my wife or I say to our son, 'You are really good at that.' Rather, we will always tell him, 'Wow, it's great that you worked so hard at that.' We put the focus on the effort *rather than on the personal identification of being* good *at something. We celebrate the triumph over the struggle, not the specific end result or being naturally good at something. Those kinds of language distinctions will lead Colt into thinking that if something's not hard, it's not worth doing, and also that he's not necessarily naturally gifted at anything, but that he does well because he puts work into whatever he's doing—The harder I work, the better I get. In that context, if Colt fails or struggles, that just means he has an opportunity to figure out how to work differently or harder the next time to be successful."*

—LARRY YATCH, RETIRED NAVY SEAL

These awards are what I call *participation* awards. The military was recognizing me for being there, for showing up, and doing my job. There are others that I got as an individual—*performance* awards—but these were awarded to everyone in my platoon who was there.

Participation awards reward *showing up*, the first and most important principle of winning; when we don't show up, we lose every time.

My youngest daughters Ella and Lea had only been swimming for a short while before they went to their first swim meet. They are both incredibly strong under the surface of the water, and their *liquid confidence* has been built up by training with me. We hadn't really spent any time learning the strokes of the surface swimmers—it's a combat sidestroke (or swimming with their hands and feet tied) only for these baby SEALs, so this was all new to them. Needless to say, they struggled to keep up and ended up coming in dead last in each of their races, but what I remember most about those swims is both of them beaming and running to me with their fourth-place ribbons. (Since there were only four swimmers, the ribbons were essentially participation ribbons.) They seemed to love them as much as, if not more than, those who got third-, second-, and first-place ribbons.

The swim coaches who put on the meet had done their job. The ribbon system created an environment in which the girls wanted to participate. The coaches understood that the girls could never grow as swimmers if they didn't want to keep coming to the practices and meets. (They also understood that if the girls didn't want to keep participating I'd probably not want to keep paying them. It's funny how that works!)

A participation award is just what its name implies: a reward for *participating*. It's a small, but critical, win in the development of any skill or sport. Life will be chock-full of ups and downs for our children, and the only way we can teach them to succeed is by first encouraging them to participate, so that they can be taught how to excel and grow. Participation is the beginning of an action.

As a performance trainer, I've seen nothing more devastating or crippling to one's ability to perform than an inability to participate in new things. It's like people reach a certain age or stage of their lives when they've already tried a bunch of things, and they feel as if their adventuresome spirit has ended. They stop trying new things. *I'm too old. I'm too out of shape. I've already failed so many times. You can't teach an old dog new tricks.* The thing is, if that dog had never stopped learning, never stopped winning new skills and capacities, never stopped participating, it would have never turned into an old dog in the first place.

Our kids will hit failure after failure and run into constant adversity if they're trying to stretch and live a life beyond themselves. If one of my daughters married some douche bag, I don't want her to stay with him because she's afraid of starting over. If my son spends fifteen years in a career that he realizes will not turn out well for him, I don't want him stay just to avoid starting all over again. We can't teach about the importance of performance if we can't get our children to participate.

Listen, I'm not saying that your children should be handed a trophy for everything they do. I've noticed that a lot of people misuse and abuse participation awards, because they don't understand them. When used properly, they can be incredibly powerful tools, but they're equally as devastating when used as crutches. If extra effort and hard work to perform only produce the same results as showing up, why even bother trying to excel? To be truly effective, participation awards must be used in tandem with performance awards; they are two halves of a whole. They must work together to get our kids to try new things and to want to excel. Think of participation awards as the launchpad, and performance rewards as the rockets. Nothing can fly without both.

> "This idea of not keeping score is completely ridiculous to me. Kids still keep score. They *know who won the game.* There's lots of value in losing and winning, and that's important for parents to learn as well."
>
> **—BRANDON WEBB, FORMER NAVY SEAL**

PARTICIPATION TROPHIES

APPROPRIATE	NOT APPROPRIATE
While acquiring a new skill	When building the skill
When they put in their best effort	When they consistently missed practice
To encourage those who don't place to keep trying	To reward everyone equally so feelings are not hurt
When passion has been lost	When someone is on fire
To get someone's attention	To keep someone's attention

"Mediocrity is a disease. As a parent, my mission is to see my two sons live and work at their highest potential—to achieve, grow, and succeed—far above the mediocrity of the masses. Sometimes that's easy to do. For example, my boys play competitive soccer, and they're both driven to reach the top of that sport. It's good to see that in them. However, they can have difficulty being driven to do the day-to-day stuff, such as homework, which is just as important and also an area where I expect them to do well. Their mom is a high school English teacher, so they're very lucky in that she has them on a homework schedule, which helps them keep up with that day-to-day boring stuff. She's good at getting them to do that, because success is more than just acing the fun parts—it's about acing the boring parts too."

—CHRIS SAJNOG, RETIRED NAVY SEAL

FAILURE IS ALWAYS AN OPTION

There is another reason people will avoid, intentionally or un-intentionally, trying new things or making changes. They are afraid of failure, of not living up to their own expectations or any-one else's. I can't stand being around or working with people like that, because when they *do* fail—because all of us do at some time or another—they can't own it and grow from it. Their inability to embrace it robs them and their team of the opportunity for growth.

My kids run for Student Council every year, and, so far, they have lost every time, which is an amazing teaching opportu-nity. It's not that I want them to lose, but since the results of the elections are opinion-based, there's a great likelihood that they will experience failure, which is a far more important skill to learn than how to be an elementary school vice president. These elections give me the opportunity to show my kids how to win regardless of how many votes are tallied.

"Okay, how well did you give that speech? How did you feel?" I asked.

"I did great," Lea said. "I went a bit fast in the middle section, but made good eye contact and engaged the audience."

"Fantastic work. Were you nervous, Ella?"

"Yes, a little bit before I walked up to the mic," she said, "but once I got there I felt fine."

"That's perfect. Now remember how you felt. The next time you have something to do that makes you nervous remember how the nerves went away and you were able to perform."

Regardless of the outcome of the election, the girls build strength and confidence as they go. They get to learn about that which they can control and that which they cannot. Their power comes from within—a renewable and unlimited source that will carry them through life.

Of course, when they lost, they both were heartbroken and tears were shed, but when I asked, "Are you going to run again next year?" they both said, "Duh, of course I am, Dad."

To me, that meant that they'd already won.

Each year, we make newer, better posters, and work to perform newer, better speeches. And we get better at managing our moods around the disappointment that comes from really putting yourself out there, really going for something, and coming up short. Remember, winning isn't beating everyone else. That's just finishing first. Winning is when you keep going after a setback. My girls saw the failure as a stepping-stone to success, a part of the process of winning. They saw what it was like to stumble and pick themselves back up. That's something that will pay off for the rest of their lives. That's what you call unstoppable—the ability to keep participating. If you keep your children focused on winning the battles of acquiring new skills, capacities, and experiences, any failure although a disappointment, is incidental, and it becomes as useful as a single step in any journey. Progress.

> "When my daughter tested for her purple belt in martial arts when she was eight, she didn't earn it the first time around. When the instructor got to her, he said, 'Madison, you're not getting your purple belt today.' She kept her composure, but when she walked out of class, she hugged me and started bawling. I said, 'Look, this is a really important lesson. You're going to earn this two weeks from now when you retest,' and she did. She had the biggest smile on her face from having failed, having worked really hard to

overcome that failure, and then having triumphed. What a
gift that was for her. It's important, as parents, to let your
kids experience failure, so they can know what it's like to
have an accomplishment. Success is the top rung of a
ladder made of failure and adversity. People say to me all
the time, 'Oh, you're so lucky to have been a SEAL. You're
so successful.' Meanwhile, they have no idea how much
training and effort I've put into whatever field in which
I've achieved success. They have no idea I was rejected
twelve times before I sold my first book, The Red Circle,
which then became a New York Times bestseller. You have
to fail to succeed, and I see so many parents who don't
let their kids fail, who don't give them the freedom to go
out in the real world and stub their toe or lose a soccer
game. That's the only way to set your kids up for success
in life."

—BRANDON WEBB, FORMER NAVY SEAL

"I learned very early on—mostly due to the bullying I en-
countered in school—that normalcy was not something I
was interested in. Think of all the bullies in school. They
were the normal kids, right? The cool kids. The ones everyone wanted to be like. They were the normal ones. What I
figured out was that no one who has ever done something
exceptional was normal, because being exceptional and
being normal are mutually exclusive. All of the success
I've had in life has always been from being abnormal. The
worst thing that someone could call me is normal,
because that person is basically saying that they never expect me to do anything of consequence or importance.
Of course, there is obviously balance to this in that being

> *completely abnormal just for the sake of being countercul-*
> *ture can also be problematic, but if I had a choice for my*
> *son, I'd much rather him be on the far end of abnormal*
> *than in the middle of normal."*
>
> **—LARRY YATCH, RETIRED NAVY SEAL**

NEVER STOP—NO MATTER WHAT

On the outskirts of Mississippi, there's a place where SEAL platoons go to hone their craft in hostage rescue. The facility rests on
about three acres of land where, on one side, there is a nondescript
house that we'd stay in as if we were visiting family, but on the
other side was a building that was referred to as a "Kill House."
The Kill House contained a labyrinth of hallways and rooms
with catwalks so that the instructors could watch our every move
as we worked to train how to clear the maze of any tangos (terrorists) and safely rescue the hotels (hostages).

"It's a dangerous job being a hostage," yelled Ross, one of the
instructors, from the catwalk as a SEAL grazed the paper image
of a hostage's hand with a 9mm round shot from his Heckler
and Koch submachine gun (MP-5) and took off running to
climb a caving ladder hanging high into an oak tree about 500
yards from where we were working.

"Slow is smooth, and smooth is fast," Ross would always say,
reminding us that when we slow things down, our minds and
bodies can better absorb the techniques. "That's the way of a gun-
slinger." Ross was one of those instructors who looked unassum-
ing, but could send a piece of lead through your brain as fast as
you could blink.

To make the training as realistic as possible we have Simunition kits, or nonlethal training ammunition—modified barrels and magazines that we put on our gun allowing us to shoot plastic paint-filled bullets. (You can't compare it to paintball, because these guys are getting shot from a gun using gunpowder.)

"Follow me through the hall," my buddy Larry Yatch said to me. "You cover down to the left, and I'll get us across." The sound of automatic fire came from the dark side of the hallway I was to cover.

Tack. Tack. Tack. Tack. Splat.

Five plastic bullets hit my inner thigh. The pain was so great that I was certain that someone had accidently went hot with live rounds and shot me. I grabbed Larry by the back of his body armor and pulled myself close as I returned fire with my MP-5 down the hallway.

Since the mission was to rescue a hotel thought to be held in the back of the complex, we had to move fast, so we kept going. I followed Larry into three more rooms, cleared them, and down another hallway before we saved the hostage and the training scenario ended.

"Range is cold," yelled one of the instructors, and I unzipped my gray flight suit to inspect my wounds.

"Man, I thought someone shot me," I told Larry as I showed him half of my nutsack and the now cherry red and bleeding welts on the skin around it.

In this kind of training, if you take a hit, you keep going. You're taught to never stop—*no matter what*. "If you trip," the instructors told us, "you get up. If you break an ankle, you keep going, and if you get shot, keep moving. How you win a gunfight is to keep moving. Once you're in the fight you never leave it. You keep going until you win. Period."

We need to teach our children to embrace life, to embrace

change and adversity. I know too many people who have just stopped trying. Some have tried a few things and stopped; others have tried a thousand things before throwing in the towel. Everyone has a number of falls they endure before they make it to the other side. The rub is that we don't know the number of tries it will take before we can be successful. For me, being a winner means always believing that you have one more try in you.

DAVID RUTHERFORD: THE POWER OF COMPETITION

I've been an athlete my entire life. My mom was a phenomenal state champion tennis player, and I started playing organized sports—football, soccer, lacrosse—from age four. Sports has always been a huge part of our family and contributed greatly to my development as a person. Back then, in the mid- to late-seventies, when I was in elementary school, if you weren't in the top three teams, you didn't get a trophy. Then it became that there were different-sized trophies for first place, second place, third place, etc., and now it's to the point where a lot of times leagues don't even keep score. In my mind, that's a travesty. Schools and parents may be trying to "protect" their children, but they are protecting them from an emotional perseverance that they desperately need to learn.

I do some seventy talks a year with some of the biggest companies in the world, and I'm always asked about how we can get people to perform at a higher level, and one of my answers is always the same: promote competition. Frogmen are members of the most competitive group of people on the planet. We will compete in every-thing—who can clean his gun faster, who can run faster, who can do the O Course faster, who can shoot better. It's crazy, but this spring of drive and competition allows us to hone our skills and be better at what we do in the real world.

That's slowly being whittled away, and it's having a very substantial detrimental effect on our kids who have been brought up in very inclusive kinds of ideals. Out in the real world, that just doesn't fly. When they get out of college and try to get a job, they can't, because they have to com-pete. And how can they start to do that when they were never taught how before? The real world is hyper-competitive, and they're ill-prepared for that. I'm a one hundred percent advocate of competition, both at school and at home. With my girls, we compete all the time for fun. Everything is a race. Who can do it faster? I want them to 1) have the drive to want to do better each time they perform, and 2) have the understanding that sometimes you're going to lose. When you lose, that failure is what ultimately shapes you into the person who can persevere in what I call the combat of life.

DEBRIEF

+ What's the difference between beating someone and winning?
+ What are the skills and capacities you want your son to win in life?

+ What is the purpose of a participation award? How can you use it?
+ How do you celebrate failures in your family and use them for collective growth?
+ Are you good at failing? Why or why not?
+ How many times do you typically fail at something before you give up?
+ How many times do you think your son should fail at something before he gives up?
+ Are you showing your kids how to be exceptional or ordinary?

8

THE ONLY EASY DAY
WAS YESTERDAY

The first time I tried to fly an airplane I was a mess. Buttons, throttles, yokes, up, down, left, right, talking on the radios—it was all too much.

"It's okay," my instructor said to me after I took us in for a somewhat rocky landing. "Don't beat yourself up. You'll get better."

The funny thing was that I hadn't been disappointed with my performance. As I landed on that runway, I was ready to try again. The fact that I had botched the landing hadn't even crossed my mind, because I knew the next day, after another lesson, I'd be better at it.

There is a famous SEAL saying etched above the grinder in the BUD/S compound: The only easy day was yesterday. Every bruised knuckle, bleeding back, and searing muscle resulting from SEAL physical training is produced underneath this sign. I used to think that the saying meant that yesterday was easy simply because it was over. Now, I think differently. Now, I know life is a series of challenges. It is as if we are, every day, charging up a mountain, and the higher we go, the more dangerous our journey becomes and the more we need to know to be successful. Now, I know that the only easy day was yesterday, simply because today is going to be even more difficult. SEALs earn their trident every day. They never cease to grow and improve. It's not a motivational statement, but a directive of care.

As shit gets harder—whether it's flying a plane or raising a child—when we manage to master it, our confidence builds. "The only easy day was yesterday" is not about dreading more work or more challenges and doing them anyway. It is about looking forward to stepping up our skill levels and becoming masters of whatever it is we are practicing. When you're in constant forward motion, when you have continuous growth, it feels as if there's nothing you can't do—every *I can't do that* becomes *I haven't yet learned that*. Every obstacle becomes an opportunity. When we stop improving every day, we have the potential to not only lose our *habit* of improvement, but to also lose our *confidence* in our ability to do so. If it's been ten years since you learned to do something new, there's a good chance you'll start believing that you no longer can.

It's important that I teach Jason to be in a constant state of growth so that growth is always an option for him. It's like a *use it or lose it* kind of a deal. So many people have lost their ability to make changes in their life, but *making changes* is a skill like any other. If you don't use it, you lose it.

I'M GLAD THAT'S IN FRONT OF ME

I didn't always feel this way. When my dad got sick, I ended up living on my own at age seventeen. I remember how hard things were as I tried to negotiate life. Luckily, I made my way into the navy. I remember thinking, *Man, that was a close one. Things could have gone really bad for me. I'm glad that's behind me!*

Then came the first screening I took to become a Marine Recon Corpsman—hours of trips in and out of the water and countless miles of running with a heavy pack on my back. The quads and hamstrings on each of my legs seized up, and the pain was so intense that I thought I was done for. I kept going, made it, and thought, *Man, I'm glad I'll never have to do that again. I'm glad that's behind me!*

Then I checked into my Recon unit and became a *roper*, the new guy who spends several months getting hammered by the rest of the platoon until he's deemed worthy to be there. I made it through and thought, *I'm glad that's behind me!*

Next came what at the time was the Marine Corps version of Special Operations training called BRC (Basic Reconnaissance Course), a three-month course that had me up and in the ocean every morning at 4 A.M. for swims complete with full rucksacks in tow. After that course was completed I thought, *Wow, I've finally made it. I'm in Special Operations now. I'm glad that's behind me!*

Are you seeing a pattern here?

In the last chapter, we talked about the importance of mental toughness in getting through a physical challenge. Mind over matter. However, it's also important that you do the work— train, progress, master—which will boost your confidence. *Matter over mind.*

There was a night during BUD/S when all I can remember is rolling around, sweating, coughing uncontrollably, and entangling myself in the 1970s psychedelic quilt that my mom had made for my older brother and eventually gave to me when I was a kid.

(My older brother became like a dad to me for most of my life. I idolized him, and this quilt has been on every deployment with me on the SEAL Teams.)

The next morning the coughing had finally stopped, and I went through the morning PT evolution of Second Phase, and by the time I was back in class I was back into uncontrollable coughing fits. It was so bad that the instructor couldn't teach because I was so loud.

"Dude!" he said. "What's the matter with you? Go to medical and have that checked out."

Finally, I was sent to medical to get a chest X-ray.

As I was walking back, one of the instructors, who could see the large X-ray envelope in my hands, said, "Hey! What the fuck are you doing walking, Davis? What's the matter with you?"

"I have pneumonia," I said, dazed.

"They drop you from training?" the instructor said with a legitimate concern for me.

"No, not yet. I've got until the next class to heal and get back into shape."

Just my luck: I had finally made it through Hell Week and First Phase and was just about to learn how to become a combat diver when I got pneumonia. I couldn't believe it. It was a gnarly setback and one that would require me to get myself back into SEAL training shape.

After Hell Week, I thought things would get easier, but they don't. I realized all the hell I had been through was just prepping me for the hell that was to come. So I stepped it up. As I got well and my training progressed, I found that my physical endurance as a SEAL increased as the intensity increased. I rose to the challenge. What also increased was my mental endurance as a father.

When I first started SEAL training, I was only able to get myself home on the weekends. During the week I needed to stay put, rest, and recover. Now, I started commuting part of the week. I even took my kids to Disneyland after an entire day of SEAL training. I would wake up at 3:00 or 4:00 A.M. to drive the 80 miles from Mission Viejo to Coronado, California. I was probably only sleeping three or four hours a night. While I was driving, I remember thinking, *Man, if I can do this, I'll be able to crush it in business when I get out. I can virtually go nonstop.*

> *"Everything comes down to how you practice, how you stay consistent, how you do it on purpose.* Natural talent *is a misconception. I wouldn't say there's no such thing as natural talent, because we all have certain abilities based on our body types, but I believe it's an extremely small percentage.*
>
> *"When my sons were super-young, my youngest would kick around a soccer ball and, one time, kicked it really hard. Everybody started saying, 'Wow, look how hard you can kick. You're a natural.' My son responded to that and wanted to impress people, show that he was a 'natural,' so he would practice every single day. He would come home from pre-school or kindergarten and go straight out to the backyard to practice soccer for hours, and then he'd come in and eat dinner so he could go right back out and practice his drills. A couple years later, when he began to play competitive soccer, once again everybody said, 'Wow, he's such a natural.' He's not a natural. If you put in the time and the practice, you're going to get good at whatever it is you're practicing."*
>
> **—CHRIS SAJNOG, RETIRED NAVY SEAL**

THIS SHIT NEVER GETS EASIER

When you adopt *The only easy day was yesterday*—or *Easy day,*
as we say—you stop chasing your tail looking for the easy life and
start experiencing the pleasure of living out your purpose and always stretching to your limits.

Having lapped the world and experienced many cultures, I
can tell you that Americans value and pursue comfort more than
most, and it's causing us all kinds of problems, both psychologi-
cally and physically (see chapter 9). I've watched my son go
through this struggle for a while. His first paid job was as an extra on the set of a Tim Allen sitcom. He made over $200 for about
an hour of work, which is great, but he learned that gigs like that
don't just keep getting thrown your way for the rest of your life. If
you keep looking for these kinds of cushy jobs, you're in for a
whole lot of heartache.

It's taken him a couple of years to recover from that experience,
to reset, and to resolve to do whatever it took to move forward. He
learned that whether he scored a good deal like the extra job or
got a raw deal like a low-paying fast-food job, *both* types of work
could push him forward every day to continuously improve. As
I write this book, Jason is working three jobs to make a go at the
life he wants. He learned that life can get incredibly better when
you quit trying to be comfortable and get comfortable at being
hard.

CONFIDENCE OR ARROGANCE?

Navy SEALs believe that, through training and education, they can accomplish anything. Does that make them confident or arrogant? There's actually a difference between the two:

+ Confidence: Believing you can do something based on your past history of performance and ability to get help.
+ Arrogance: Believing you can do something even though there's nothing in your history that indicates you can.

I've trained my kids in the activities in which I excel and in the way I live my life. They've watched me and, through my lessons and exercises, have become confident in many activities. Sometimes, however, they believe they can do what I do, simply because they're my children, and I have to shut them down. My son will say, "Oh, I can do that," and I have to say, "No, you can't. You haven't done anything like that before. I love your confidence, son, but that's being arrogant. Be careful here, because you can get hurt." SEALs know that confidence increases our ability to build, while arrogance can bring that ability to a grinding halt. And knowing the difference can save your life.

TAKING OFF THE TRAINING WHEELS
SO THAT THEY CAN EAT SHIT

I remember the first military freefall (MFF) parachute jump I did without any instructors holding me. We jumped at an old, and what should have been abandoned, airfield that had neither grass nor asphalt on which to land. Instead, it had what we called *grassphalt,* a deceptive blend of weeds and cracked concrete. I liked regular freefall jumps and would have been content to just keep doing them for a while. At least long enough to get comfortable with it. However, just falling comfortably out of the plane wasn't going to cut it. We needed to go beyond, so the new tasks came quickly:

- Before I really got comfortable with falling and flying straight, the instructors added a back flip to it.
- Once I did that, they added a full rucksack to strap to my legs.
- I barely managed that when they strapped an oxygen mask to my face.
- Just barely comfortable with the idea that I may not die, they said, "Time to take the training wheels off," and had me jumping in the black of night. (The night of our night jumps was bereft of any wind, which isn't a good thing, because the act of heading into the wind helps slow you down before you touch the ground.)

In SEAL training, the instructors are quick to take the training wheels off for two reasons:

+ We've got shit to get done, and it's for the trainees to figure things out.

+ I think it's a bit fun for the instructors to watch their
buddies eat shit. Since none of us were very good at
landing in the daytime on soft grass, there was nothing
left for us to do but ride our chutes in and take the beating. "Yeah, get some," one guy yelled as he watched his
buddy go ass-over-tea-kettle across the grassphalt for a
good 30 yards.

As a SEAL, 99 percent of what you learn to do can't be done
right away—freefall parachuting, four-hour night navigation
dives, high-level marksmanship, running 200 miles in a week.
You don't look at anything you can't do as being a fixed character
trait. You're taught that all training is something to be mastered
and each day is an opportunity to add to our present skill level.
(Truth be told, even though I'm a qualified military HALO [high
altitude, low opening] jumper, I still look forward to the day when
I can go back to the airfield and learn to simply parachute.)

> "People come to me all the time and say, 'I'll never be a
> good shooter.' You know what? If you say that, you won't
> be. The first thing I try to do with students like that is to
> get them to break their negative mindset, because if they
> don't, they're doomed to fail. Their success has nothing to
> do with being talented or not talented. It has to do with
> them owning their practice and putting themselves in a po-
> sition of power. I encourage them to be what I call an MVP
> Shooter using meditation, visualization, and positive think-
> ing. I practice the same kinds of exercises with my sons."
>
> —CHRIS SAJNOG, RETIRED NAVY SEAL

PEAKING IS FOR PUNKS

Working hard, training, and getting better at something allows us to grow. It's not about making two hundred bucks an hour. It's not about making a shitload of money in your twenties so you can coast in your thirties. It's about accepting that life is meant to be a challenge, that it should be hard all the time, every day, and that work is hard, too—they do call it "work," after all—but it can be rewarding, allow us to grow, live in the present, and look to the future. In my experience as a human performance practitioner and coach, people often tell me that they want to be exceptional, but they don't want to put in the effort. Just like everyone wants to be rich, but they don't want to do the work, study, and train every day for that level of comfort. People want to *be* something without doing what's required to get there. Becoming successful—a SEAL, a father, a man—takes years of dedication and sacrifice. You have to prove yourself every day. Sick, hurt, or tired, you show up (as discussed in chapter 7) and do the job. No excuses. Just consistent results every day.

This pursuit of comfort and luxury is something that has been made up by marketing executives. Luxury and comfort are not goals or ideals—they're distractions. They're shiny objects designed to get you to chase them, and if you let them, they'll become all that you pay attention to. This growth thing, this constant improvement, isn't meant to be one and done. It's a continuous process that requires patience and maturity. We must teach our sons that if they accept that there will always be challenges in life and that they'll always be on a path for improvement, they can spread out those luxuries and comforts, schedule them around the moments that make up their lives, and settle in for the long run.

The only easy day might have been yesterday, but tomorrow will be a better you.

CHRIS SAJNOG:
INVEST IN YOURSELF EVERY DAY

After I had been in the military for a year or two, I was talking to my mom about this exciting thing I'd discovered called *mutual funds,* an investment program that utilizes a concept known as *compounding*—if you invest a little bit of money each month, that money will grow. She said, "Yeah, yeah, Chris, that's how we made our money, through mutual funds." I remember sitting with her right there and thinking, *Wow, I had to learn this lesson on my own?* That's kind of crazy that my parents didn't explain finances or the power of investment to me as a young boy. As a father, I really wanted to make sure that I taught my sons about the importance of financial stability and planning.

I recently read a good book called *The Compound Effect* by Darren Handy. In that book, the author talks about two people having to choose between getting $3 million up front or getting a penny that will double each day for thirty-one days. It's so interesting to see what happens to the person who chooses the penny, because for the first fifteen days, it seems like the growth is minimal—two pennies, four pennies, eight pennies. You're at Day 15, and you've only got $160, and the other guy has $3 million and is living in Tahiti drinking margaritas. However, by Day 31, that penny has become about $10 million.

I wanted to teach my boys, who were nine and eleven at the time, that lesson. I had them both read a book about the importance of practice, because I'm a trainer and teach firearms, and I believe how you practice is so much more important than what it is you're practicing. I wanted them to understand that, so I had them read a book about the importance of practice, and told them that if they finished it and wrote a little report on what they learned, I'd give each of them $100.

They both took me up on the offer, finished the book, and wrote the report. When I sat down with them to discuss the book, I had a hundred-dollar bill in one hand, and in the other hand I had a penny. I said, "You can take the one hundred dollars right now, as promised, and you can spend it on whatever you want." I actually made them tell me what they were going to spend it on, because I wanted them to be excited about it. Then I said, "Or, instead, you can take this penny and double it for sixteen days." (I wasn't going for thirty-one.) The younger one, being younger, I guess, had that $100 I held in my hand spent already. He didn't care about the penny or what he would get if he waited. However, my older son took the penny. He said, "I don't know how much money I'll have in the end, but I know you, Dad, and I know you're trying to teach me something." And after sixteen days, my oldest son ended up with more than $200 to spend on what he wanted.

In the end, both boys learned the same lesson. They learned about the importance of compounding and of investing—not just financially, but how investing in your training and in yourself, how doing a little bit each day, can build and build, whereas those who reach for too much too soon can end up with less in the end.

DEBRIEF

+ What are you better at today than you were a year ago?
+ What challenges have you overcome to reach a goal?
+ What challenges have stopped you from reaching a goal?
+ What personal limits are you currently stretching?
+ Are you confident or arrogant? Why?
+ Do you pursue comfort or purpose?
+ Do you currently train in any discipline? How has it affected your confidence?
+ In what training is your son engaged that will build his confidence?

9

GET OFF YOUR ASS

They had me locked up. I couldn't get out. The panic started to set in. I had been caught and was now paying the price. Perhaps what made it so difficult was that there was only a single pane of impenetrable glass between me and freedom. I could see the grass, the trees, and almost smell the wind. It was torture.

I couldn't have been more than five or six years old and was sitting in front of the sliding glass door of our townhouse experiencing what I can only describe as a blend of rage and terror. I slammed my face onto the ground and started beating my fists against the thin carpet that covered our dining room. *I needed to get outside.* I've long since forgotten what I had done to warrant being grounded by my mother, and my captivity only lasted half a day, but not being able to get outside where I could once again run, climb trees, and get muddy had left its mark on my psyche.

This is who I am. Then and now. I am me when I'm outside running, surfing, swimming, hiking, and anything else I can think of that involves an increased heart rate and fresh, unconditioned air. When I was growing up, my family would refer to this condition as the Curse. I didn't sit still. I was the kid in church who would be twitching his face in impatience when the congregation was singing hymns. During my toddler years, my older brother, Grant, often had the duty of keeping me under control. When we were out of the house he'd have to use one of those kid leashes to keep me from running off, and when the family did the unthinkable and tried to sit me in a high chair at a restaurant, I'd resist the restraints of the chair by throwing my food everywhere, an energetic act that eventually warranted a family policy of taking turns with me in the car while the others ate. It felt like I had a rocket burning up inside of me blasting with anxiety and anguish. I simply needed to move.

Luckily, because I lived in a townhouse area surrounded by grass fields, endless sidewalks, and multiple parks, I had ample time and space to play, and that's exactly what I did—from morning until night. My parents knew I had a ton of energy, and I thank God that they chose to manage it by simply allowing me to burn it. Because of the great outdoors and the access I had to it, I became fast, energetic, and extremely happy. Without it, I probably would have grown up frustrated, troublesome, and extremely sad. Though my family and I still joke about my Curse, I've come to find my energy level and desire to be outdoors more of a blessing. For me, being active is a way of life and has driven my overall health and happiness.

I meet plenty of men who have the Curse. Many are SEALs. They're happy when they are moving, going, and doing, and since leaving the Teams, they've found livelihoods that help them to keep the energy flowing in a healthy and productive way. However, many men have not. They work in tiny cubicles and on cluttered desks. They have a half hour for lunch, if they're lucky, and the only heart-pumping activity they do is walk from their office to the car, and then from their car to their front door.

The predominantly knowledge-based economy of today's world requires a dependence on brainpower rather than physical power, and this desk-bound, computer-based environment is having a detrimental effect not only on our bodies and minds but on how we parent and interact with one another. If we're to live a good life and lead our sons to do the same, we're going to need to get off our collective asses and get our adventure on.

> *"My family would go to the movies, devour a large popcorn, nachos, and soda, and then after the movie, we would drive home, except my dad would run the ten miles back like it was nothing. I've had a lot of friends with dads who would come home from work, watch TV, and then go to bed. Never were they active with their kids, and most of them were out of shape, too. Not my dad. He would be active with us and then go run ten miles afterward."*
>
> **—JASON DAVIS**

RELATIVE ASSESSMENT

For years after I left the Teams and began working in the corporate world, I couldn't figure out why there were no gyms, showers, and locker rooms in my office buildings.

"When and where do people work out?" I asked Belisa.

"They don't, dumbass," she said. "Working out isn't part of normal people's workday."

When we measure or evaluate our situation or status according to those around us, it's called *relative assessment*. Well, here's what's around us, according to the President's Council on Fitness, Sports, and Nutrition:

+ Only one in three children is physically active every day.
+ Children now spend more than 7½ hours a day in front of a screen (e.g., TV, video games, computer).
+ More than 80 percent of adults do not meet the guidelines for both aerobic and muscle-strengthening activities, and more than 80 percent of adolescents do not do enough aerobic physical activity to meet the guidelines for youth.

Most people may not be aware of their inactivity, because they've become surrounded by it. I've always been the oddball who would run to or from dinner parties to get my miles in. "That's crazy that you do that," I'd hear constantly. Now I know why. Laziness has become the rule rather than the exception. Chances are that if the people around you don't think you're crazy for being so active, then you're probably not being very active. You may need to get off your ass!

Movement is essential, not optional, for health and well-being. The navy knows this. When I was conducting sniper support for my platoon's ship-boarding (legal pirating) operations, I was getting flown from ship to ship so that I could use their helicopters as airborne sniper platforms. Every ship had exercise bikes, elliptical machines, weights, and treadmills, and many of the ships kept some of these high-dollar pieces of equipment out on their decks, exposed to the corrosive salt air, so sailors could be outside and move.

After spending all night sitting in the door of a helo watching my platoon climb on, tear up, and take down ships smuggling cargo out of Iraq, I cherished the time when I got back to the ship and rode a stationary bike in the middle of the ocean with my headphones on, watching the sunrise. It kept me sharp and sane and gave me the ability to sustain these types of operations for long periods of time. It may seem counterintuitive to do mentally exhausting work and then add a physically exhausting exercise as a method of keeping your energy level high, but it works. Energy begets energy. (For more on "self-regulation," see chapter 10.)

Men are meant to be active. We are built for mobility. We need to move our bodies enough to maintain muscle, flexibility, and cardiovascular fitness as well as mental acuity and overall good mood. Just because we no longer *have* to spend all day hunting, gathering, and surviving doesn't mean that we *shouldn't* spend time hunting, gathering, and surviving. The yearning to be outdoors is inside us, and when we don't satisfy that need in productive ways it can do more than lead to levels of fatigue and fatness. Not being active can be detrimental to our mental health and day-to-day quality of life.

THE DISEASE OF BEING STUCK INSIDE

Have you ever been to the zoo and noticed how the bears or tigers pace back and forth when stuck in their enclosure? That's what carnivores developed and bred to cover 50,000 acres hunting and searching for food look like when their landscape has been chopped down to 50 yards or feet.

Imagine the stress and anxiety that animal might be feeling as his internal motor, thousands of years of natural drive, keeps spinning at a rate that is geared for great distances but now has nowhere to go. It's like simultaneously pressing the gas and brake pedals down to the floor and never letting up on either.

If you have an active and adventurous soul like I do, you're probably feeling the same way. Every bit of anxiety, nervous twitching, and sipping of alcohol I've used to deal with my high-RPM internal engine being forced to function in an enclosed space is my form of pacing. It's like half a heartbeat that presses on our chest just aching to get out, pushing us toward some nasty habits and even nastier moods. We spin out. We get anxious. We take on unhealthy lifestyles in order to cope—overeat, drink too much, do legal and illegal drugs, watch excessive TV, cheat on our wives, anything to make us feel alive, anything to lift that brake pedal so our gears can turn freely. I call this the Disease of Being Stuck Inside.

I find it funny how, in our society, we are always trying to get kids to sit still, to be quiet, and to listen in class when we're all designed to move. Adults who've run their energy levels so far down that they now require caffeine to simply make it through their day are the ones who create stagnant environments and expect kids to simply "Sit still and pay attention!" We are creating environments that teach our kids *not* to be healthy and active. Research shows that physical inactivity is associated with all kinds of emotional and behavioral problems. According to the Centers for Disease Control and Prevention, people who are physically active not only tend to live longer, with a reduced risk for heart disease, stroke, type 2 diabetes, and even some cancers, but also keep their thinking, learning, and judgment skills sharp, as well as reduce their risk for depression. Unfortunately, according to the Physical Activity Council, the year 2014 showed the highest percentage of inactivity in the last six years, and Americans continue to struggle with a commitment to physical activity.

Simply put, when parents aren't active, their kids aren't either. I see it with my own eyes: parents who sit around, which teaches children that idle time is lazy time; parents who come home from work and automatically turn on the television or head to the computer, which teaches children that screens are go-to leisure time activities.

Listen, video games have their place. For me, as a kid, they were a wonderful part of the equation as they stimulated my mind and gave it something to chew on. They're fun, and they've taught me about tenacity and the ability to concentrate for long periods of time in order to work and solve problems. They taught me how to fail and try over and over and over again. However, because I was spending plenty of time being active outdoors, I didn't become obsessive or locked onto video games as a kid or locked onto technology as an adult. My outdoor physical activity kept me loose. It breaks my heart when I see adults and children incessantly leashed to their phones.

If I'm not adequately stimulating myself, I can be anxious, depressed, stressed, restless, and short-tempered and have problems sleeping. For a long time, I thought there was something wrong with me. I searched long and hard to figure out how to manage this Curse of mine. I went to all kinds of doctors and studied and read everything I could find about it. Hell, I even started knitting. Eventually, after a lifetime of intermittent suffering, I figured it out.

"I just have more energy than most people," I told Belisa as if I had discovered a secret.

She looked at me and said, "You think?"

There's a whole world out there to explore. I know we're all busy and time is at a premium for many families, but we need to reorganize our commitments so that we can find the time to *move*. Our lives, and our children's lives, really do depend on it.

SEAL PUPS

Close to where we used to live, there is an ancient Acjachemen village known as Panhe, which means "place by the water." It's over 9,500 years old and is where the Juaneño/Acjachemen Native Americans lived back in the day. In an effort to preserve its heritage and prevent the sacred grounds from getting plowed under by yet another toll road, the village hosts an annual Earth Day celebration.

A few years ago, I had taken my two youngest girls there to learn more about the village and the people who lived there. One of the booths they had set up was manned by an older Native American gentleman. He had long salt-and-pepper hair, scraggly sideburns, and a weathered face, and wore a faded pair of blue jeans and a leather vest adorned with an assortment of beads. We were in the presence of a true local.

He sat next to a basket filled with water and what looked like weeds. As the girls and I were cruising past his booth, he startled them by asking, "Would you girls like to learn how to make rope from plants?"

"Oh, yes, please!" they replied with their usual enthusiasm.

As the girls bellied up, he said, "This is how Special Forces make ropes in their survival training."

They immediately looked up at me for confirmation. I glanced down as he was showing them what a finished product looked like and said, "Yep, that sure is."

As I sat there watching this amazing man share his traditions, crafts, and knowledge with the girls, I noticed how engaged they were. I thought to myself, *Now that's a useful and exciting skill to learn.* Then it hit me: Why in the hell don't I form a group and teach kids not only survival skills but also sniper hides and underwater knot tying, and even show them how to install grommets in their swim fins, so that they can connect them to their backs for conducting amphibious reconnaissance missions?

Boom! The seed was planted. I stole the name SEAL Pups from a family activity that the navy conducted for the kids of Special Warfare families and slowly began to build my own program. I began to take the best of Special Forces, firefighting, rescue, and law enforcement to inspire confidence, skill, and functionality.

After a few years of competing with the demands of soccer, swim, and piano lessons, the idea began to die. Finally, Belisa and I said, *Fuck it, we're going to make it happen.* We pulled the girls out of every conventional activity and told them that we were going to do SEAL Pups.

"Girls, we're going to teach you to be badasses!" I said.

"Oh, yes, please!" they responded.

As a sniper instructor, I obtained certification as a master training specialist. It's a fairly difficult certification to get and basically means that I'm a subject-matter expert in course and instructor development. As we developed our SEAL Pups program, I began to use this knowledge to develop both instructors and curriculum that were of high quality and extremely useful for matters of both survival and badassery. We do underwater hunting (spearfishing and lobster diving), ocean swims, river crossings, water rescue, diving, rock climbing, building evacuation, map-and-compass land navigation, hiking and patrolling, sniper hides, and many, many other activities.

One of the few regrets I had as a father was not being able to do these types of things at this level with Taylor and Jason when they were young. I was constantly away training and deploying. Now that I'm home, I'm working to fill in some of the gaps and create a unique and powerful experience for not only my kids but others as well.

ARE WE BRED TO BE BORED?

We all require different levels of activity to stay sane and healthy. My experience is that most Navy SEALs will represent the high end of that spectrum—they need a lot of activity. Anytime we're "penned up" for long periods of time, we're not likely to just sit still and wait it out. Ask a SEAL what the most dangerous type of SEAL is, and he'll quickly reply, "A bored one."

One time when I was a sniper instructor, we were wrapping up a course in the middle of the desert east of San Diego. We had finished cleanup early, and since the trucks weren't scheduled to pick us up until the next day, we were left with four or five hours of daylight to burn.

Another instructor named Johnny, a laid-back, avid fisherman who spoke with a stereotypical Californian accent, said, "Yo, we need to get rid of some of this extra ammo. Let's roll out to Range Five and burn it up."

Assuming that "burn it up" meant our usual massive fully automatic firing squad, I grabbed a couple of M-4s (standard military assault rifles), a bag of magazines, and some shooting gloves to protect my hands from the desert sun. The ride out to the range took about twenty minutes. We had some pretty mellow reggae music playing in the government 4x4 truck, and I was starting to feel a bit sleepy by the time we got there.

"Let's get this shit done and go back and grab some beers," Johnny said.

"Sounds like a plan," I replied as I shook my head to revive myself.

The students had loaded up the extra ammo, so I hadn't looked in the back of the truck until we got there.

"Holy shit, dude," I said. "That's a lot of ammo to shoot up. We're going to burn up our barrels."

"Burn up our barrels?" Johnny said. "Who said anything about shooting it up? We're going to light it on fire with an incendiary grenade. It'll be fucking awesome."

(As I write this, I'm a bit embarrassed to confess that I replied, "Hell, yeah, it will be. Let's do it!" Neither one of us considered what might happen when a very large pile of ammo started to cook off. I blame the reggae music.)

It took about thirty minutes to pile the ammo up just right to ensure that it all burned. Johnny grabbed the incendiary grenade (an extremely hot-burning grenade designed to melt through and destroy anything), pulled the pin, and said, "Fire in the hole," as he placed it on top of the pile of ammo.

At that moment, it finally occurred to us to put some distance between us and what would soon be a burning pile of bullets. Johnny headed to the truck to get it started while I hung back to make sure the wood under the incendiary grenade caught fire. Once it did, I felt the sense of urgency that comes with lighting a pile of bullets and started a slow jog over to the truck.

Then, like popcorn in a popper, the bullets started to crack off, one after the other.

Bang!

"Oh, shit, dude. They're already going off," I yelled to Johnny.

Bang!

Another round went off, and I could hear it spin right past me, nearly hitting me. Since the bullets weren't traveling down the barrel of a gun, they wouldn't have the spin or velocity required to fly effectively. As a result, they tumbled dangerously and made a sort of buzzing sound as they flew past.

"Oh, shit, Davis, get in!" Johnny yelled as he did a doughnut to spin the truck bed my way.

Another *crack* went by and sent me into a dead sprint toward the truck, where I literally dove into the back as the rear tires started violently spinning to get us the hell out of there.

"Teams and shit," Johnny said as he switched the mellow reggae over to hard rock and sped back to camp.

Like I said. Boredom and SEALs. A dangerous combination.

FORGING BONDS

In SEAL training, Surf Torture randomly repeats throughout all phases of instruction. It's an evolution of unknown duration in which the instructors have the students lock arms and walk out into the cold Pacific Ocean until the water is just below their knees.

"Take seats," the instructor calls out over his bullhorn, and, in unison, an entire class of SEAL trainees sits down in the water.

"On your backs," the instructor calls out, and immediately the entire class is submerged under the water with only the tips of

ACTIVE BODIES *MUST* EAT

A common assumption about Hell Week in BUD/S is that the instructors don't feed us. On the contrary, during that five-day period of constant motion, we eat *a lot.*

Every six hours, SEAL students get as much nutrition as they can stomach, a balanced blend of carbohydrates, protein, and fat—no fad diets or special supplements, and most of us stayed away from caffeine during that week. The message is not to eat until you puke but rather to eat until you have satiated your body with wholesome foods jam-packed with good nutrition. I grew up eating shit like canned ready-to-serve meals, sugary cereals, and processed foods (what I call "sheep food," because as a society we herd up and head to the troughs, or store shelves, for this stuff), so during the eight-plus months I spent at BUD/S, I had the opportunity to reset my eating habits. I began to look at food simply as the fuel that it is. Life as a SEAL promotes a fit and active lifestyle. (That's not to say I don't tear up the occasional plate of nachos.)

It's the same policy I use at home with my kids. We have a *don't finish your plate* policy—we eat until we're full, and then we stop. And if you don't want to try something, you don't need to. Find things you like that have the proper balance of protein, carbs, and fat, and stick to them. If you make a big deal about food, there's a good chance your kids will, too.

their toes, the caps of their knees, and their faces remaining above water.

The torture occurs every time the water recedes and the cold subsides, because you experience the discomfort of getting hit by cold water over and over again. It would be like jumping into a cold pool and never being allowed to get used to it, just the cold shock over and over again.

Why are SEALs asked to lock arms? Because the increase in resolve and collective protection that comes from locking arms with the guys next to you is immeasurable—and biological. Stressful and intense situations can release oxytocin (sometimes called the *cuddle hormone* or *love hormone*), a hormone that is secreted by the pituitary gland, a pea-sized structure located at the base of the brain. This hormone is known for its ability to increase the feelings we have toward those with whom we are sharing the experience—the bonds we have with them. Human beings need other human beings to survive.

These evolutions forge bonds—the brotherhoods—between Navy SEALS, Army Green Berets, Rangers, firefighters, and police SWAT teams who rely on one another in times of extreme stress. When I was working Hell Week as an instructor, we'd get guys to quit by simply not allowing them to lock arms during the evolution. We'd sit them in the water alone and watch them drop like flies. Bonding is a powerful ally.

As a father, I take this idea of bonding in a stressful environment to heart. From the time my kids were born, they've been active with me—climbing, hiking, free-diving in the ocean. We spend time together engaging in higher-risk activities so that we can learn to rely on one another and produce bonds that can last a lifetime.

Keep in mind that when I say "higher risk" I'm not talking about tossing them out of a plane or anything like that. I'm just talking about getting off the beaten path and going beyond the playground. Too often, we stick to the ordinary, which can only produce ordinary experiences.

In Eric Blehm's book *The Last Season,* which is about a lost park ranger in the Sequoia National Park system—one of my favorite places to go—he says, "It is estimated that 99 percent of the visitors to the parks' backcountry stay on . . . designated tracks, which represent less than 1 percent of the parks' wilderness acreage." That's why when I take my family into a park we look for the road less traveled. We work to go places and do things that are extraordinary. This pattern of ours makes for some terrific bonding time.

A few years ago, the entire family headed out to a local hiking spot to do some climbing. We got about a quarter of a mile down the trail and came to a staircase—actually a dried-up waterfall. We could only see the top third, where the "steps" passed from our right to our left and descended down a steep canyon that must have been carved out over the thousands of years the waterfall had been flowing.

Each step of the waterfall stairway was steep, and my daughter Lea was only three or four years old at the time, but I had a climbing rope and equipment with me, so I thought we'd be able to manage it well enough. I was the lead climber of my platoon, so this wouldn't be the first time I led a group through a climb.

The down climb started off easy enough. We broke from the trail and entered a mix of dirt, bushes, and a dried-up creek bed that led to the start of the waterfalls. Everyone was able to pass on his or her own. So far, so good.

As the group continued the down climb, the granite walls that were the steps of the waterfall stairs became steeper and higher, forcing us to pass Lea back and forth to each other, lowering her down from one ledge to the next. Though the steps got increasingly taller, we never had to break out the ropes to get Lea down; her outstretched body was just long enough to be her own little rope as Jason and I alternated between lowering her down by her hands and catching her by her ankles. He'd lower her to me and then quickly scramble past me so that I could lower her down to him. By the time we got to the bottom, we had become a well-oiled machine.

At the base of the waterfall, the rock flattened out into a very cool little canyon with mini rock walls to climb on. We spent a few hours climbing and having fun as a family. The only incident we had was when I had climbed myself into a bit of a pickle and actually thought that I might take a fall. I sent everyone around the corner and out of sight before I made my move to get down. I didn't want them watching me just in case I came off the wall. I wasn't high enough to die, but I was certainly a contender for a compound fracture. I thought it better for future family climbing if the kids didn't have to watch their dad sand-dart into the ground. Luckily, I was able to quickly make my way off the wall without any dramatic incident. So far, we were still good. It wasn't until what I thought would be the easy part that we got into a bit of trouble.

On the way back up, having had our fill of climbing, we decided to take a different route and skirt the waterfall from the top side. At the time it seemed reasonable, possibly even responsible, but as we gained elevation things began to get a little sketchy. The trail thinned out; a combination of erosion and circumstance pushed its edge toward the working end of the cliff. We cautiously skirted our way toward the top, but about halfway up I realized that the consequences of a slip had upgraded from bruises and breaks to death. It was time to rope up.

There's something about tying a climbing rope to your kid to protect her from death that changes the game and, no doubt, releases that oxytocin. Should one of the girls fall, she wouldn't die. She'd end up dangling, but she'd be scared shitless. My wife, Belisa, got nervous and started to tear up. She didn't lose it completely, probably because she wouldn't risk scaring the girls. The entire family's mood became serious. It felt like more of a rescue operation than a weekend family hike.

We spent the next hour cautiously working like a team, crossing crevices with the most precious cargo imaginable. Though I ensured that we were all safe the entire time, it still felt like a life-or-death situation. Adventure is always relative.

As we came to the final ledge, that last bit that took us from *Holy shit, we're fucked* to *Holy shit, we made it,* I glanced over to the opposite side of the canyon, the place where we first departed the trail that 99 percent of the park's visitors would most likely stay on, and spotted a family just standing there staring at us.

"Don't worry, we do this all the time," Belisa said. "We've got some screws loose."

"No," the father replied. "We thought it was the most amazing thing we've ever seen. You guys are awesome. It's a great show of teamwork." Then that man and his family just sat there and watched us, never asking if we needed any help. I guess from the outside looking in, it must have looked like we knew what we were doing.

We finally made it back to the trail and back to our truck. I remember the drive home being fairly epic, not because of any more physical challenges but because I could tell that we had all drawn closer as a family, as a team.

"I was totally not on board for this! I had no concerns as we went down the riverbed and having to help the girls down because their legs weren't long enough to crawl. However, on the way back, when—literally—the trail was crumbling under our feet, I was scared and pissed at Eric. I knew he didn't put us in danger on purpose, but the fact was that we were. I couldn't show how upset I was, because I didn't want to scare the girls, but my heart was racing, and I wanted to cry, but that wouldn't do any good. We worked together, used our ropes and harnesses, and once I saw it was going to work, my fear went away, but I was still pissed that we were caught in that position. Still, as a SEAL, Eric was able to assess the situation, figure out what we needed to do, and get us all to do it without anyone freaking out. I was proud of how we worked together that day. It was a defining moment for our family. (Needless to say, this was not the last time this has happened. I would say more often than not when we are hiking we have to use some sort of rope to get us down. The last time we had the dog with us, which was fun.)"

—BELISA DAVIS

Adventure is relative. *Extreme* for a kid doesn't have to be a double back flip with a motorcycle. It could be your son standing up on the ledge of a climbing wall and you saying, "Okay, now lean over the edge and let go of the rock. The rope has you. I have the rope." It could be dirt biking or parasailing or skateboarding or whatever physical activity your family finds exhilarating and new. It doesn't matter what you do to get your children out of their comfort zones. Just get the fuck up and out. Your son will thank you for it. And so will your body.

WHAT IF MY SON AND
I LIKE DIFFERENT ACTIVITIES?

All of my kids enjoy the outdoors and certain levels of activity, but I don't think any of them have the same need for it as I do. (Apparently, I've successfully bred with much more stable psychologies than my own.) This leaves a bit of a gap between what I want to do and what my kids want to do, which can present a challenge in keeping active as a family.

My ex-wife, Stacey, would always say to me, "It's not about you, Eric." She's right, and it means I've got to spend time doing what my kids like to do and not always expect them to do what I want. (I've bought my son two remote control planes and a boat that I don't think I've ever let him fly or drive, nor has he cared. I'm that dad who buys toys for himself and just puts *To Jason from Santa* on them.)

These gaps in preference are real, and there must be a compromise, but it's important not to confuse them for a bit of laziness. There are many times when I know that my son and I enjoy the same activities, but it can still be a struggle just getting him out there. He doesn't want to get up, get ready, and head out the door. He's feeling lazy or has gotten locked onto a video game or TV show.

Forcing activities is very different from *nudging* kids to do activities. I've often used the same technique with Jason that I discuss in chapter 7: I work to just get him to show up. I'll say, "Jason, you don't have to surf. Just get all of your stuff, and we'll get to the beach." Once we get there, he suddenly wants to surf.

> When planning family activities, discerning between apathy and lethargy is an essential parenting skill. Remember, that applies to ourselves as much as our sons.

BRANDON WEBB:
EARNING YOUR TRIDENT EVERY DAY

You have to earn your Trident, your SEAL pin, every day. I remember a guy at SEAL Team 3 who had an attitude problem. He was a really smart guy but had a chip on his shoulder, and he became adversarial with his platoon leadership. He started mouthing off while he was on probation. (There was a six-month probationary period back when Eric and I were SEALs, which I wish they would bring back.) You can have your opinion in the SEALs, but you can't be a jerk about it, and his behavior became a pattern. The guys didn't want to work with him, so they kicked him out. They sent him back to the navy. Just showing up wasn't enough to make him a SEAL. He had to earn that.

My friend plays in the National Hockey League—he's a bona fide All-Star—and he told me that there were plenty of guys playing hockey that were better than he was and better than a lot of the other guys in the NHL, but they just weren't nice guys; people didn't like working or playing with them. Scouts knew this, and those guys never got picked up to play pro hockey. Same thing applies to life and parenthood. Just because you showed up for that music recital doesn't mean you can coast or back off for a few days. You still have to be there earning your parenthood every day, and you have to teach your children to be good people and team players.

A few years ago, I took Jackson to the SEAL training pool, and all these First Phase SEAL students were doing push-ups in their white shirts. I looked down at them and saw him, the guy who had been kicked out. He had to go through BUD/S all over again, and he ended up making it. I think he learned something. He went on to become a really good guy and to have a good reputation, but, man, going through SEAL training twice wouldn't be my choice as the way to do it.

DEBRIEF

- ✦ List the bad habits you engage in when you're not active or intellectually stimulated enough?
- ✦ List the bad habits your son engages in when he's not active or intellectually stimulated enough?
- ✦ Do you accept that health and fitness are critical to living a good life?
- ✦ How much exercise do you get in any given week?
- ✦ What are your go-to activities after work and on the weekends?
- ✦ In what ways are you setting an example for your son with regard to health and fitness?
- ✦ What physical activities have you done with your son that have created bonds between you?
- ✦ What areas of your life and your son's life do you think are affected by inactivity or lack of intellectual stimulation?
- ✦ What will be the next physical activity you do with your son?

10

RESPECT A FIGHT

There's a SEAL hand-to-hand combat exercise called the Box Drill that has everlasting effects on the way you approach any kind of fight. The drill begins when the instructors bring you to the corner of a large room that is marked off by a shaded white box on the floor. The room is all black—black walls and an assortment of black curtains and barriers—with heavy-duty rubber padding on the ground, and on the side opposite your box, there is a door on a fake wood wall, much like you would find on a Hollywood set. They explain to you that within the box in which you are standing—and only within that box—will you be safe from any harm.

"Okay, Eric," an instructor told me, "your job is to get from where you are, in the safe zone, all of the way across the room and out that door. There's no time limit and no rules. The drill starts when you see the first threat. Go."

I waited for something to happen, but nothing did at first. I didn't know what to expect and was trying to get a game plan together when eventually five or six thugs with chains and bats sauntered into the room. *Oh,* I thought, *it's gonna be an ass whooping, I get it.* The guys used for this drill come from a place called X-Division, which is where the SEAL students who quit, got hurt, or otherwise did not make it through training go. These guys are usually not in a good mood.

The fighting instructors handpick the biggest ones out of each crop to use for training drills such as these, and as the gang loomed toward me, they began with verbal harassment and quickly became more aggravated and aggressive as they drew in. The famous words of comic Ron White went through my head: *I don't know how many of these guys it would take to kick my ass, but I knew how many they were going to use.* It was go time.

I sprinted, dove right at the guys, and started hitting and punching them. Meanwhile, the guys, all of whom were wearing hoods and protective gear, were completely unfazed. They shoved me, hit me, and slammed me into the wall. The melee continued until the group rendered me ineffective, and one of the instructors blew his whistle and told me to head back into the white box to reset.

"Eric, you good?" one of the instructors asked. "Do you want to try that again?"

Though I couldn't see any possible way I'd fare better on the next go, I quickly replied, "Oh, yeah, let's go again."

The whistle blew, and I charged them. I faked a punch to the guy to my left, pivoted, and nailed the guy to my right, who stumbled back a bit, but by the time I was getting ready to hit him again three more dudes had come around behind me and hit me in the back of the head.

Back to the white box I went in defeat.

This routine of me diving into the fight and getting my ass handed to me repeated itself a few more times. Somewhere on the fourth or fifth try, I finally opted not to dive straight into the group. I waited and tried to figure out a better plan while I caught my breath. As I was breathing and thinking, I noticed that one of the attackers left the room. I looked up and said, "Hey, where'd that guy go?" And when the X-Division thugs turned and looked at the door, I ran at them again—and got my ass kicked again.

I was back in the white box, trying to figure out a new game plan, when another guy left the room. The instructor said to me, "Davis, you have all the time in the world. Remember, there's no time limit."

Cool, I thought, *got it,* and I instantly attacked the remaining guys again and got my ass kicked again. This went on and on, and each time the instructor reminded me that I had plenty of time to complete the drill.

Suddenly, it hit me: *There's no time limit.*

I decided to wait it out, and after a while another few guys left the room. When there were two dudes left, I went for it one more time, but they were able to pin me, and we reset once again.

Finally, I just sat there on the floor of the white box, and after a while one dude left, and then the other guy left. I looked around, confused. The instructor yelled, "Get to the door," so I bolted for it, and finally made it out. The drill was over.

After the drill was complete, I chuckled to myself: *What the hell was that for?* I hadn't gotten any better at fighting, and there was no real end to the confrontation. The guys just left. Had I failed the drill? After all the SEAL students finished their Box Drills, all with about the same results, the fighting instructors explained to us that the purpose of the drill was to beat into you—literally—just one thing: Whenever you're in a safe place, you should stay there.

Why is that? Because any fight can lead to death. Any fight can become a fight for your life. Any one of those guys in the Box

Drill could have had a knife or a gun. If I knew my attackers couldn't come into the box, that it was a safe zone, why would I leave to go engage them? It was a combat lesson that could also be applied to our personal lives, when we were at a mall with our family, for example, and saw questionable characters in the parking lot. Would we *SEAL up* and confront them or wait and keep our family safe in a store? Wait it out, they said. What if we were at a bar and some idiot wanted to take a title shot with a SEAL? Would we really risk life, limb, or our careers to defend some antiquated notion of manhood? No, they said with great sincerity, walk away. They told us that out of all the fight training they did, the Box Drill—with its lesson of strategy rather than reaction—had probably already saved the most lives, and we believed them.

NOT EMBRACING THE HATE

When I was a little boy with red hair and freckles that looked like they were splattered onto my face and arms, I was no stranger to getting picked on. All of the usual verbal stuff such as "freckle face" and "carrot top" was thrown at me, and one idiot even came up with "period head." There was also some mild physicality, such as overly aggressive play fighting, and one time in church a big kid whacked me too hard on the head with a cardboard candy cane.

Like most other kids, I hated my bullies and how weak they made me feel, and because I was never taught how to fight, like most other kids, I thought I had to take their shit from time to time. (It was only once I got older that I realized that they probably didn't know how to fight either.) Anger, frustration, and hate would pulse through me if I watched a bully pick on someone and I hesitated to defend that person for fear that I'd start a physical fight.

It wasn't until I pursued the ability to fight through adolescence and the SEAL Teams and became more powerful myself that I began to see bullies for what they are. They aren't the strong ones. They're the ones who are too cowardly to get what they want without having to hurt or take from those who are weaker than they are. I realized that they no longer had the power to make me do or feel anything that I didn't choose. I became free.

A sign that Belisa bought me when I was a SEAL hangs in my house with two SEAL Tridents affixed to it: *The true soldier fights not because he hates what's in front of him, but because he loves what is behind him.—G. K. Chesterton.* Belisa gave me that sign because she knew I didn't want to ever let anyone force hate within me again. As a boy, I thought the way to defeat bullies was to become more powerful than they were. It wasn't until I was an adult that I realized I already was.

"Last year, a friend of my oldest son, Jackson, was being made fun of by a bully. Jackson stood up for his friend and wound up taking a punch in the face for him. Jackson is a straight-A student, a bass clarinet player, and an athlete. He's not a jock, but he's just a good-hearted kid, and he took one for his buddy. I said, 'Look, it's so important that you stand up for people, because what you did was a good thing, even though you got punched.' He and I had a really long, cool talk about it. He said, 'Yeah, Dad, it was the right thing to do.' It

was *the right thing to step in. He wasn't looking for a fight. I don't even think he punched back. He stood up for what he believed in, and I told him that when you do that, it sets a good example for others and is a good habit to develop. Now, my most challenging thing with Jackson is how to have the sex talk with him, because he's thirteen, he's got a girlfriend, and I'm terrified."*

—BRANDON WEBB, FORMER NAVY SEAL

LEVEL OF FORCE

In our fight training, SEALs are taught to use three levels of force based on what an opponent *deserves*:

Level I: Gentle. Hands on, grabbing, and moving with a light level of force, as if to break up or prevent a fight between two people. You're working to control the situation without escalating it.

Level II: Firm. Medium to hard face strikes, take-downs, and choke holds. A drunk guy at a bar who gets aggressive and touches you may *deserve* to get hit with your hand.

Level III: Fight for your life. The moment you fear for your life, you unleash everything you've got. You may go instantly to III, or you may be in a Level I scuffle and the person won't back down. Level III means you have to end this fight now!

Adhering to this level of force is the expected behavior for the stronger person or unit of the conflict, who has a higher level of responsibility to prevent any escalation of the situation.

IDENTIFY. AVOID. DETER. SEEK. DEFEND.

We call hand-to-hand combat training CQD (close quarters defense) or CQB (close quarters battle), and it's organized around the notion that every fight can lead to a fight to the death. Therefore, when Navy SEALs find themselves confronted by an opponent or adversary in a potential conflict, they follow a certain protocol not only to ensure their safety but to ensure they win:

+ Identify the threat
+ Avoid and increase distance
+ Deter or barricade
+ Seek help
+ Defend

Identify the threat: This is also referred to as *situational awareness*. To be a SEAL is to be constantly scanning the environment. What do the people around me look like? How are they dressed? Do they fit the environment? What's their attitude? Does anyone look concerned? Threatening? When I enter a space, I look for immediate threats and orient myself so that I am prepared for conflict, which means that I am in proximity to an exit or entry point. Michele, my mother-in-law and a very well traveled international humanitarian, often teases me about this. We took a family trip to Sudan in Africa, and she saw me doing my thing and told me it was okay to relax. I explained to her that I wasn't stressing out, that I've simply gotten into the habit of scanning and noticing my environment tactically like a photographer would aesthetically. He's in the habit of noticing light and color. I'm in the habit of noticing weapons and intention. It's all art! (I don't think she bought it, but my point was that being aware and having your head on a swivel doesn't mean you're nervous and uptight.)

Avoid and increase distance: If you notice anything out of the ordinary—a person acting suspiciously—or if anything goes wrong in whatever environment you find yourself, your first order of business is to get out of there. Most fights, danger, and conflict can be avoided well ahead of time if you've properly identified the threat. In most SEAL missions, we work to avoid *contact,* meaning we work to get in and out without any disturbance. (Getting contacted is often considered mission failure.) Therefore, when I see anything that looks out of the ordinary in a situation, I leave—like a proactive version of a Box Drill. People assume that because I'm a SEAL, I should fight. On the contrary: Because I'm a SEAL, I should win. And usually the best way to do that is not to fight, and especially not on somebody else's terms. Trouble is easy to find if you're not paying attention.

Deter or barricade: As we all know, sometimes trouble comes looking for you, no matter how much you try to avoid it. If you're in a tactical situation, barricade yourself with anything you can find—tables, doors, etc. This concept of barricading is what they taught us in that Box Drill. The white box represented a barricade. It could just as easily have been a mall or a store. Remember, safety is your number-one concern.

In a classroom situation involving a bully, you can barricade yourself with kind friends or be in the presence of an adult. I teach my kids that bullies are a lot like wild animals that have found their way into your school. It's not my kids' job, nor are they trained, to handle bullies safely or in an effective manner that will work out for them. I expect the school to protect my kids both physically and emotionally. That's the school's job.

Seek help: SEALs always look to tilt the odds in their favor. We're never looking for a fair fight. Though we're small in number, we've learned to leverage and deploy tactics and technology that ensure our success. We want to see through the night as well as through walls. We've got badass Army Rangers or Air Force Pararescue serving as our QRF (Quick Reaction Force) on standby, ready to bail us out of any situation. We look for help anytime and anywhere we can.

Years ago, when Taylor was young, I was at the playground with her. There were two boys, one was probably about six years old and the other maybe four, sitting and playing in the sand. At some point, the younger boy decided to take the older boy's truck from him, march off, and play with it by himself. The older boy was visibly upset and went to his father for help with the situation. The younger boy needed to learn how to problem-solve and communicate, and the older boy needed to learn some conflict resolution. The boy who had his truck taken had essentially been bullied, and how he handled it would likely set the stage for how he'd handle conflict with others for the rest of his life. I remember thinking, *Wow, what a great teachable moment here.* Unfortunately, neither boy wound up learning shit.

"No! You don't let anyone take your stuff away from you," the father of the older boy told him. "You walk over there and punch him right in the face. If you don't learn to stand up for yourself, people will be taking your stuff for the rest of your life."

I grabbed Taylor's hand and left. When we got to the car, I looked back at the playground to witness a six-year-old using assault and battery to solve what could have been a very simple resolution. Both fathers present had the opportunity to teach their sons the most effective way to act, and both failed to do so. Somewhere along the way, our culture has taught men to deal with frustration, anger, fear, and failure through aggression. It's become such a go-to reaction that we'll do it even when it makes no sense. We'll act like those little irritating dogs with unchecked aggression barking and growling at the bigger ones as they walk by. Seeking help in situations that are escalating toward physical violence doesn't just mean finding someone bigger to protect you. It also means finding someone smarter who can teach you how to handle it on your own. SEAL training has taught me that to start a fight means that you've exhausted all intellect and/or self-control.

Defend: We won't always be able to avoid a fight. Therefore, there will be times when we must prepare for conflict. Leaning on the principle that every fight can end in death, SEALs take this reality very seriously. If your son has surpassed his intellect and skill, if he has avoided, barricaded, and sought help unsuccessfully, he may have no other choice but to fight a bully who is about to hit him. Remember, fighting is your last resort. When people fight, it's typically the result of intellectual exhaustion; it means you've surpassed your capacity to take care of the situation with your acumen and know-how. It should never be a default setting.

My son, Jason, has trained in martial arts off and on throughout his life. He's smart, quick, and strong, and fighting has been a very uncommon occurrence. It'd be easy for me to take a stand and say that I think everyone should learn how to fight, but really that is up to you. I will say that to fight effectively takes a lot of training and time. It's what's called a *perishable skill*. Though I could make a strong case for focusing on awareness and avoidance in every circumstance, I'd be remiss if I didn't remind you that there is evil in this world. I often say that the chance of any single bad thing happening to someone is slim to none, but the chance of nothing bad ever happening to someone, I believe, is zero.

> "Eric has a very pragmatic outlook on parenting. He looks ahead and makes decisions based on what could happen. Every decision can be life threatening in his book, and that hasn't always been easy. I can remember being exasperated many times when he would keep going on and on about something I found to be trivial. Only to him it wasn't. He sees things ahead that most of us would never see. I think this comes from all his SEAL training and how SEALs are always looking for ways that things can go wrong, how the smallest thing could ruin an operation. He always looks ahead and not always in the now, which can be super-frustrating—especially when he ends up being right! He always has a best-laid plan, and if things go that way, great, and if they don't, then we make adjustments and get back on track. He isn't super-militant with the kids, nor does he come down hard on them. I am the one who brings down the hammer in our house. However, if Dad has to step in, everyone knows it's really bad! One thing that drives me crazy is that he has the patience to sit out anything or anyone. I think it comes from sniper school. His patience level is ridiculous, as is his ability to ignore whatever it is that is going on around him. If he decides he is only going to focus on one thing, then that is it. It's getting done no matter what."
>
> **—BELISA DAVIS**

IT'S ONLY REAL FIGHT TRAINING IF YOU'RE TAUGHT TO RUN AWAY

Situations come up all the time in which I have to assess potential threat levels as well as the likelihood of the threat materializing. Case in point: We had just spent a couple of days camping in the redwoods just east of Santa Cruz, California, with our close friends Scott and Aubrey Seymour and their kids—two much-needed days of whittling, hiking, and tying off big rope swings using climbing ropes and harnesses so that we could launch the kids into the air.

On our way out of the mountains and back home, we decided to stop at Santa Cruz's famous boardwalk to ride some of the rides and grab some food. As we were walking back to the parking lot toward our trucks, which were stuffed with gear, I spotted him. Someone was at the back of my pickup bed poking around. I had just reached out my arms to turn everyone around when my Italian wife and my friend's redheaded wife, both beautiful, little tiny women, said, "Hey, what the fuck are you doing in our truck?"— full f-bombs in front of four kids as they leaned forward and started toward the dude. As a group, we went from detection right to defense in a matter of seconds—not our finest moment, tactically speaking. We now had his attention. We were engaged.

The women broke out ahead of me, and because there wasn't time or opportunity to turn the group around, Scott and I pushed out ahead and told them to hang back a bit with the kids. Luckily, whatever plans the guy may have had to steal something out of my truck or any ideas of getting aggressive were squashed as Scott, two feisty women, and I closed in on him. He hadn't taken anything and became passive, so Scott and I directed him to leave.

Afterward, the group was a little confused as to why I had

tried to turn them all around. I mean, Scott's a pretty good-sized dude and in shape, and I'm no slouch. Both of us can take care of ourselves, so why should we just let someone get into our stuff? Where was the justice? What's the point of being a SEAL? It was a cool moment since we had our kids there to talk about the Box Drill—if you're in a safe place, stay there. That man could have had a gun or a knife or had friends watching from a distance ready to come in and help him. Cornered, he could have become dangerous. I explained to the kids that it wasn't about being scared of the guy or protecting our stuff, it was about keeping our family and ourselves safe. It's important to think big picture. Create distance and call the cops.

In this particular instance, we experienced a training failure. I hadn't taught my family how to handle a situation like this, and I failed to see the threat early enough to divert the group before engaging with this guy. Usually, I'm way out ahead on this stuff and would have diverted my family without them even knowing what I was doing. That wasn't the case this time; I had gotten complacent. Because of this, we got close enough to him that we gave him the power to determine whether or not to physically engage. The possibility of an attack was real, and I made the determination that it would be more effective to quickly close the space between us so that should he so much as sneeze I'd already be between him and my family. I went to Level I and became the aggressor.

Knowing when and where to attack or retreat is an intuition that SEAL fight training built into us through experience. During training, the fight instructors routinely had us stand face-to-face with an attacker at various distances and then take turns initiating the first move. This developed our ability to assess distance threat and taught us that if we used that first move to escape the situation, it put us at an incredible advantage.

WITH FRIENDS LIKE THESE . . .

Children are often taught to stay in groups for safety. This is good advice, but it only works if your kids aren't hanging with dipshits. Often it can be the people we are around who cause most of our troubles. I've had a few too many buddies act like a fool. I always tell them that next time, I'll just let them get their ass kicked if they're the ones who failed to control the situation, ending up in a fight. The last thing you want is your son ending up in a confrontation because of the actions of one of his friends.

When I was in the box and saw those guys walk in with chains and bats, I thought that the drill might have been to see if I'd lean into the fight. I thought the instructors were testing my courage. Therefore, I dove into it, not because it made any strategic or tactical sense but because I thought that was what I was supposed to do.

The twelve-year-old in me heard nothing but *Hit the ball, Davis, don't be afraid.* Not charging at those guys would have been like not diving for that catch, and I was afraid I would have heard *Why in the hell didn't you dive?* from my fighting instructors.

I got my ass kicked repeatedly that day, because I was acting like an inexperienced child and not a seasoned Navy SEAL. I allowed myself to be bullied into a dangerous situation, not because I didn't have a choice but because I didn't know I had a choice.

Respecting a fight is all about power—the power to influence your environment, and the power to choose. It's about teaching our sons how to manage conflict and giving them the knowledge and skills necessary to deal with it, on their terms, when it comes.

I'm a SEAL who doesn't like to fight, and I don't feel bad about it at all. Why should I? We call the men who work to resolve conflict and manage those who cannot *peacekeepers,* and that is who I want to be. They're no more passive than a navy destroyer sitting off the coast, its crew members biding their time until the next fight for their life that they're prepared for but hope will never come. Today's world is filled with all kinds of bullies, from the playground to the battleground. Most of these assholes aren't worth your son's time. By avoiding, distancing, barricading, and seeking help, he can strip them of their power and be not only safe but in control of the situation.

I've taught Jason to not be a victim. I've empowered him to choose when he's going to fight and what he's going to fight for. For Jason, it's not only about his own safety and protection, or that of his friends and family, but also about the safety and protection of everyone around him. When our sons know how to respect a fight, others can learn to respect one, too.

LARRY YATCH:
SELF-REGULATION AS A LIFELONG PROCESS

I was a tiny, skinny kid who was not a good athlete, so I got picked on a lot in my childhood. I was bullied horribly from second grade through fifth grade, and then from freshman year through sophomore/junior year in high school. What I learned very early on was that fighting was easy. I fought on a regular basis and got into trouble, but fighting never solved the bullying; it just stopped it for a moment. What *did* stop the bullying was when, instead, I didn't react at all. If the bully made fun of me and I didn't respond to him. If I created a stoic exterior, he got bored. It wasn't fun for him to pick on a kid who didn't react. I learned through that experience that the way you win is not always through physical fighting but through *self-regulating* your reactions, by not giving bullies what they wanted, which was very difficult to do, because often what they said to me did hurt my feelings.

It's important that we teach our children that everyone around us has different levels of impact on our lives. For example, our parents have a long history of caring for us and impact our lives directly, whereas strangers on the street, or on the Internet, have never shown care for us and have little direct impact. As a parent, we must empower our children to know that they alone control the power of judgment. We need to teach them to safeguard the judgment of those who care for them while ignoring the judgment of those who do not. This becomes a practice in mental and emotional self-regulation that should continue throughout their lives.

Over the course of my life, I got good at this kind of self-regulation, and because I wasn't a very good athlete, I tended to self-regulate through whatever came my way— exercising, being on the wrestling team, bullies. All of those hurdles exercised that self-regulation "muscle." I tell people that I really became a SEAL in the seventh grade, because everything I did from that point on was to build up that ability, which served me well and made me ready once I hit SEAL training. My seventh-grade brain wanted to join the Navy SEALs for two reasons:

1. I figured out that the best way to make sure that no one could bully me and that I, more importantly, could get rid of bullies all across the world was by being a SEAL, because, in essence, the people the SEALs go to fight, especially nowadays, are 100 percent bullies. They use power to project force to hurt people who have less power. I couldn't stand for bullying to exist.

2. All those years of kids saying I was no good, all the bullying that goes around in your head long after the bullies are gone, leaves a nagging thought that maybe the bullies were right—you might not be worthwhile, you might not be good, you might be weak. I joined the SEALs to prove to myself, not to anyone else, that I was capable, that I was tough, and that I was a worthwhile person.

The thought of doing a combination of those things—completing one of the hardest, toughest things in the world and getting to go after mass-murdering bullies? I'm in, sign me up, and point me in the right direction.

DEBRIEF

+ How did you feel about avoiding a fight before reading this chapter?
+ How do you feel about avoiding a fight now?
+ List the four things that should happen before someone defends himself or herself physically.

+ Define power.
+ Use the five phases of a fight to describe how your son might handle a bully at school. Describe how those phases can empower him and produce confidence.
+ How do you handle bullies? What do you do when someone cuts you off on the road? Yells at you at a ballgame?

11

TAKING BACK WHAT'S MINE

Over my sixteen years of military service, my family became accustomed to me being either on the road training or overseas on deployments and secret missions for months at a time. When I left the SEAL Teams in 2008, I was eager to redefine and deepen my relationships with my children and finally have some quantity time.

Unfortunately, it seemed like I was the only one who was ready.

Although we were physically together, my kids seemed perpetually distracted. Boyfriends, girlfriends, work, school—their life was getting in my way. More than a month would go by and my son, Jason, and I would hardly say one word to each other. Though our physical distance had never been closer, in terms of our relationship, it seemed as if we had never been farther apart.

Even when you're doing everything right—leading from the front, keeping up rather than catching up, and developing a wonderful space filled with stories and shared experiences between you and your son—that space is always leaky, at least in my experience. If you fail to keep filling it over time, it can become empty. Or worse, filled with something else. The trick is to notice and acknowledge that space you share before the emptiness is insurmountable, and that's what I planned to do. It was time to take action.

Because I had spent a lifetime engaging with Jason and being active with him, and I knew it to be an effective strategy, it was time to do it again. I needed to take my kid out of the house to rediscover that risk-taking spirit of adventure, and I needed to do it away from the distractions of everyday life. And so on Jason's eighteenth birthday, I lured him into the High Sierra with the intention of throwing him off a cliff.

After six hours of driving, we reached the gates of Kings Canyon National Park, home of some of the largest trees on the planet. A few miles in, we found a dirt road and started to follow it, driving for miles on rugged off-road 4x4-only terrain. I didn't just want to get away, I wanted to go where others could not go. I wanted an adventure, and if that meant him and me getting stuck and hiking out, so be it. One way or the other, our time together would be unforgettable.

After two more hours of driving, we found a hill that looked unclimbable. We went for it and found ourselves atop an amazing mountain overlooking a sea of painted trees, endless valleys, and distant cliffs. I got out of the truck and stood by Jason hoping for a miracle—wishing that he would once more lean his head on my shoulder and say, "Love you, Dad," the way he did as a child when I'd return from some far-off place and take him to do something fun.

Suddenly, out of nowhere, there was a large *crack*. It sounded like the supersonic *crack* a bullet makes when it flies over your head. My training kicked in. Certain we were taking fire from an obscure sequoia-tree-hating terrorist cell holed up in Kings Canyon, I scanned the environment for threats. There was another *crack,* and this time movement caught my eye.

"Jason," I said, "look, a tree is falling!"

In what seemed like slow motion, a massive tree listed like a sinking ship and then hyperaccelerated to the ground, splitting itself in two as it crashed around its sturdier neighbors, and in a flash, that dead space between us filled. We had been transformed from Eric and Jason back to father and son. Nature, once again, delivered an experience that both he and I could share.

We got back into the truck and kept driving. We noticed granite rocks just off the trail. After a few minutes of scrambling about, we found them: a perfect set of terraced stone walls that looked as if they were up against the end of the world. It was late, so we decided to eat dinner there, at the edge of infinity, and forgo the cliff drop until the next day. (I've often thought it strange that people regularly wait an hour for a good table at a restaurant but seldom will drive 7 miles off-road to eat a $7 backpacking meal in nature. It's too bad that the herd tends to stick to its pasture.)

We finished our food and set up camp. There were no sources of light or sound in the sequoias, so we decided to build a partial shelter in the back of the truck so that we could sleep under the stars and just be. I know the simple act of sleeping outdoors doesn't seem that extreme or even exciting, but if it's not something you do every day, the unfamiliarity can create a feeling of bonding and closeness. It's like you're depending on each other to be safe.

The next day, we set to work scouting out potential climbing and rappelling routes and going over our climbing gear—finding the anchor points, tying the knots, rigging Jason's climbing harness, setting up the rappelling equipment. All of these activities helped me to reclaim my place of authority, control, and, most of all, trust for Jason. I don't care how many YouTube videos your kids have watched, if it's their first time crossing over the working end of a cliff with nothing more than their dad's knots and an *attaboy,* you've just become the coolest dad ever.

As our children near adulthood, they will change, their needs will change, and our bonds with them will change as well. The time Jason and I spent in the woods redefined our relationship— we reconnected not only as father and son but as friends. And as they go on to create their own lives and live them on their own terms, we want to keep an open line so that love, information, and knowledge can continue to flow freely.

It's easy to get caught up into thinking that you need to do something extreme or expensive—or even extremely expensive— to create these kinds of moments and memories with your sons, but, in general, that's really not necessary. Just a few weeks ago, for example, I went on a day hike with my buddy, his sons, and my youngest daughters, Ella and Lea. We drove thirty minutes to a nearby trail, hiked maybe two miles in, and busted out a small backpacking stove to cook up some lunch. Right as we were finishing up, my buddy's twelve-year-old son looked up at him with a huge smile and said, "This is the best thing I've ever done for lunch in my life!"

I looked at my buddy and smiled. "Man, that's all it takes," I whispered.

Just getting outside can trigger these kinds of reactions from our kids. Grab a couple of water bottles and some trail mix, and just get out there. For my family, it's always been Mother Nature herself, the source, that's given us the best kinds of joy and the most memorable experiences. And she doesn't require any special talents or toys. All you have to do is step out of your house and into hers.

"When that big sequoia tree that had been standing there for longer than I have existed decided to fall right at that moment, scratching and taking some smaller trees along with it until it hit the ground, my dad looked at me and said, 'Happy birthday, buddy!' It was one of the best camping trips we have ever gone on, and it is still my favorite birthday."

—JASON DAVIS

THE O COURSE

In SEAL training, you run the O Course just about every week. About 200 yards away from the Pacific Ocean, the O Course consists of some two dozen obstacles set in the soft sand, including parallel bars, a tire obstacle, a low wall, a high wall with rope, a low crawl under barbed wire, a cargo net, balance logs, *Hooyah* logs, a monkey bar ladder, and a slide for life, an extremely tall structure with flat decks in the middle that force you to hang off the side as you climb. The course is designed to build your strength, skill, balance, and determination to hold on tightly and not fall—a culmination of all your training.

Every time I ran the O Course I felt like I had gotten a little bit tougher, a little bit more courageous, and a little bit more confident. With each new run, it slowly transformed from a course with worrisome obstacles from which I could fall and die to one with simple climbs that I would run up and over without thought. Over time, the O Course made the difficult routine—my grip got stronger, my confidence greater. *Attacking* obstacles, as we say in the Teams, would become an attitude that would serve me well for the rest of my life and, I would make sure, my children's as well.

THE DIRTY NAME

The O Course has a particular obstacle that's called the Dirty Name. It's a sequence of two horizontal logs that are just high enough and far apart enough that most people, under normal circumstances, can't make the jump. Many SEAL students, myself included, didn't make it the first time, because in order to be successful you must disregard all sense of space, distance, height, and concern for your own personal safety. You must do nothing less than heave yourself as high and as far as you can. Imagine having the opportunity to become a SEAL, which, for most of us, is a lifelong dream, and there is a log suspended just out of reach that's going to stop you. You have no option but to toss your body at that log over and over again, and in doing so, you call that damn log every name in the book.

Eventually, multiple instructors gather around to watch you bounce off it—depending on the day and who you were as a student, they might be taunting you, instructing you, or feeling for you. Since there is little to no technique involved, there is not much instruction going on. All they can do is make sure that you keep trying and reinforce that what you are doing is right. It takes faith and a no-quit attitude to eventually stick it to that son of a bitch. For many of us, there is no other option than to exhale all of our air upon impact in hopes that we stick. In the end, some do, and some don't. Effort does not guarantee success. It only removes the guarantee of failure.

LOOSENING THE KITE STRINGS

When Taylor and Jason were kids, Belisa and I would take them to the SEAL training ground to practice on the O Course with Zoe, our German shepherd, all the time. (I remember the base police would walk up to us and tell us we couldn't have any dogs on the beach, but when they realized I was a SEAL, they'd say, "Oh, you guys can do whatever you want. Have a nice day.") Taylor and Jason grew up on that O Course. They would do some of the obstacles on their own, and we would help them with others. I couldn't let them go up and over the very dangerous obstacles, simply because if they fell they would die, so they spent their time on those from which they could safely fall without getting badly hurt. I miss the days when I could keep them off the deadly obstacles.

The hardest part of parenting has been watching Taylor and Jason transition into adulthood. All their lives, Belisa, Stacey, and I have worked to help them grow and experience failure, but we were always there to catch them and keep them from hitting the ground. We buffered their failures in order to let their confidence grow. We could tell them *No, that's too dangerous* or *Get off that, you're going to get hurt.* If they made the wrong choice or got into too much trouble, we could exercise our right to swoop in and pick them up. They still had time to learn cause and effect.

Now that they're older and making their own choices, we can no longer stop them from taking too big a risk or tell them *Get down from there!* like we used to. They must be left alone to make their own choices and experience the unfiltered consequences of them, what we call the Proofing Phase, or Completion Phase, of their training. Any picking up we do—bailing them out financially or enabling a lifestyle beyond what their current education and skill set can support—will only hurt them and prevent them from building the skill, strength, confidence, and courage they need for the war of life. It'll give them a false sense of security and produce lethal levels of hubris. Putting your adult kids in an obstacle course, tying strings to them, and lifting them up and over every time they come up against an obstacle fails them rather than helps them. Not only will they not develop the muscles, toughness, and endurance that come from running the obstacle course themselves, but, perhaps even more dangerous, their intuition about what they can and can't do also won't develop. They will be robbed of the opportunity to experience a life that is commensurate with their choices.

As your children reach adulthood, it's time for them to walk their own path, and the truth is, neither of you has ever been where they want to go—you are walking point together. If they want to travel a path that your experience tells you is the wrong direction, you're going to have to let them go and hope that the lessons you've taught them over the years stay with them. It's time to test their ability to put being effective over being right.

We've all come across adults who suffer from arrested development, those who are destined to live a life of dependency, can't seem to stand on their own, are always asking for a handout, and seem to consistently make bad choices and engage in hurtful behaviors. They never truly grow up. At some point, we have to cut the strings and let our children become what SEAL instructors call *sand darts,* a term used to describe students when they fall off a high obstacle and smack the ground when they fall, but I suggest it might be best to limit that to when they're still young enough to bounce!

PAPER TIGERS

When I was in sniper school, the instructors warned us not to become a *paper tiger,* someone who graduated from sniper school, earned the title of "sniper," but failed to maintain and further develop his skill as one. I look at the word "father" the same way, as a commitment to continuous evolvement as a leader and source of knowledge for our sons. The moment we stop developing, we become fathers only on paper.

RALLY POINT

It wasn't until I started working on this book that I realized how much time I wasn't spending with my oldest children, Taylor and Jason. When they turned eighteen, Stacey, Belisa, and I started to pull back, as we should, and let them go out on their own. However, soon we noticed that they were making ineffective decisions that would put them on trajectories resulting in undesirable situations. We want our kids to try and fail, but it's important for them to be able to understand those lessons of failure so that they can continue to grow. It's as if they were to break their leg—we want to be the cast that ensures they will heal stronger and straight. We realized it was time to reengage and reclaim the team. It was time to return home, to our rally point—the safe place we all come back to if we get engaged by the enemy and are split up.

Because they were now adults, any guiding and coaching that we provided had to be done on their terms. When they were younger, we could just alter their environment or command them to stop or start doing something. Now, it had to be their choice. The game had changed. Our job was no longer to tell them what they can and can't do but to help them become observers of situations that their actions produced. We may not approve of all their choices, but we can certainly support them in their efforts to determine what's best for them.

During any journey, on sea, air, or land, we call this *getting your bearings*. It's what you do to find out where you are on the map—assess your direction of travel and determine if it is still taking you where you want to go. I've seen Taylor get herself in over her head financially and then buckle right down and work two jobs to correct the situation. I've watched Jason poke at multiple career paths and quickly realize that any action would beat no action and move accordingly. To watch both of them experience life and success and recover from any failures without complaint or hesitation has made me as proud as I can be. It's not about making the *perfect* choices but about *learning* from the choices that we make. So long as they can evolve, they will remain unstoppable.

THE BROTHERHOOD

From time to time, I'll run into a SEAL buddy I haven't seen in years. We'll go for a beer and be sitting at the bar, and he'll reach his arm out and put it around my shoulder, because—even though we've been estranged or haven't seen one another for a long time—the experiences we had, the groundwork that was laid in SEAL training, everything we've done, has forged a lifelong brotherhood. We have a shared beginning.

Fathers and sons, too, have a brotherhood that stems from a shared beginning, from the time the sons were babies throughout their journey into manhood. I feel like I have been growing up right alongside Jason for the past twenty years, and as we move into the future and he comes into his own, I hope to be collaborating with him as much as leading him. Our experiences thus far are just the beginning. We've got the rest of our lives to continue on this journey together—to lead, to learn, to evolve—because there's still a long way for both of us to go.

If there's one thing I want you to take away from reading this book, it's that there's absolutely no reason to think, *Shit, look how this guy raised his kids, and I blew it! My kids are already gone. They're in college. They're adults. They have their own kids.* It's never too late to reconnect, reengage, and rally up. It's never too late to say *I love you* or *I'm sorry.* The best part about making mistakes is finding solutions—and maybe redemption. Remember, Fourth Phase is forever. This parenting thing is still going. Get going with it. *Hooyah!*

JASON DAVIS: FATHER AND FRIEND

My relationship with my father has changed slowly over the years because he is now out of the Teams. When he was a SEAL, he was more of a "distant father," and I don't mean that in a bad, salty way, like *Dad's missed yet another birthday.* I actually get a little irritated when I watch movies where the children of the hero cop are mad at him because he is gone all the time for work. I've never felt that way toward my dad, who not only didn't come home at night but was gone for six-plus months at a time. I was not telling him how angry that made me, like these kids in the movies. My dad was across the world, and the info we had most of the time was just the continent he was on, but he was saving the world in my eyes. And as I was growing up, there would be times when I would look around and think how nice and safe everyone felt and that that was because of my dad and his friends and others like him.

This can all sound awesome, but I'm not saying it wasn't hard, either. There was crying from everyone pretty much every time he left. I, of course, would try to compose myself for my family, whether I felt I had to or because my dad told me to take care of my sister, which I believe is why I'm actually really good at holding my composure today.

Now that I'm an adult, my dad is both father and friend to me, and, depending on what we are doing activity-wise, those roles can easily change order. My father's advice and knowledge is some of the best I know, and to this day, if he issues a rare command, whether in a high-risk situation or not, I will immediately follow it, because I truly believe that it would be in my best interest to do so.

DEBRIEF

+ In what ways are you a paper father?
+ Do you lift your kids up and over life's obstacles, or do you tend to let them handle them on their own?
+ What are some ways you've hampered your son's growth by supporting him too much?
+ If your relationship with your son fades, what will you do to get it back?

Acknowledgments

Hell Week's got nothing on writing a book, and I couldn't have done it without the support of my team:

Belisa: For being my partner, my friend, my confidant, my moral compass. For always supporting me in all I have ever done, even when that meant you were on your own for months on end. For always believing in me. I love you.

Stacey: We were just kids ourselves when we became parents, learning as we went. I am proud to have grown with you. No matter the situation, we always remained dedicated to our kids, and, most importantly, we always remained friends. Our kids are lucky to have you as their Mom, and Belisa and I are fortunate to call you our friend.

Taylor, Jason, Ella, and Lea: I always wanted to be a dad, but until I had all of you I never knew how much I would cherish being a father. I am honored by the trust you've put in me to lead and guide you over the years. Not a day goes by when I am not full of pride and love for all of you and who you are becoming. Every day I strive to be the man you deserve. I love you.

Marc Resnick and the team at St. Martin's Press: The words "I support our troops" slip off the lips of many Americans without thought or action. I thank and applaud you for putting action behind those words. The stories of the men and women of the military belong to the American people. Thank you for giving us a voice.

Dina Santorelli: For getting "me," for knowing when to push and when not to. For believing in this book and encouraging me to "show" more. For taking my calls and answering my e-mails, even when I am sure you didn't want to. Your positive attitude and dedication to getting this book written have been immeasurably valuable.

Ellen Scordato and Stonesong: Thank you for all the behind-the-scenes support and guidance throughout the publishing process, and for having my back.

Mom and Dad: It is a good thing I was a good-looking redhead or else you might have sent me back. Thank you for always encouraging me; for the hours spent at the pool watching me swim; for taking me camping, fishing, and hiking; for understanding my love for the ocean; for forgiving me when I skipped school to surf (once or twice, or sometimes daily); and, most of all, for always making me feel loved. You were the safety net that allowed me to keep jumping for greater heights. I love you.

My big brother, Grant: You have always been like a dad to me. I have always looked up to you and always will. You walked point for me and shared every lesson you learned, even the hard ones, helping me to become a man. Your dedication and love for your family have inspired me over the years and continue to be the bar for which I strive.

My big sister, Lori: I couldn't have asked for a better sister. You have always supported me, worried about me, and prayed for me.

You have never been quick to judge, and you unselfishly love all of those around you, especially your family. Your kindness knows no limits, and your strength is amazing. You are unconditional love.

Michele Del Conte: For hitting me on the head and telling me when I am in the wrong, and for opening your heart to me and my two oldest kids from the get-go. I always joke that it is every parent's worst nightmare to have their daughter marry a divorced redheaded Navy SEAL with two kids—only it wasn't a joke! The example you and Bob set when it came to how to raise kids is remarkable. I have learned so much from you and am so thankful to have you as my second mom and to be part of the Del Conte family.

Toby Hecht and Greg Scharnagl of the Aji Network: For cracking the code and revealing the secrets of life and for sharing those secrets with me and thousands of other ambitious professionals. It is the knowledge you gave me that allowed me to see and understand the principles I used as a SEAL and sniper instructor. Without you, neither this book nor my success could exist.

Justin and Sandy Scopaz: For your love, encouragement, and support. Justin, just knowing that you thought what I was doing was a good idea was all I needed to go for it. Sandy, your spirit and passion as a mother and a friend have inspired and guided Belisa and me. Thank you.

Brandon Webb: For being my teammate and one of my best friends throughout this journey. We've leapfrogged throughout our careers, from one command to another, from the Teams to "real life" (whatever that is). After twenty years, it's plain to see that our friendship has kept us connected, and will keep us connected for the next fifty.

Larry Yatch: For being my leader and one of my best friends, both in the Teams and out. I don't know a finer person than you.

David Rutherford: For being an inspiration to all. Thank you for making the positive and motivational message of the SEAL Teams available to the world.

Master Chief "M": For teaching me about life and leadership. Your impact on my life is greater than I've ever told you.

Chris Sajnog: For being a leader, friend, and fellow sniper instructor. Your professionalism has always inspired me, and continues to inspire me.

Mike Ritland: For Indy and all of the knowledge about high-performing dog behavior, and your witty "Team Guy" way of explaining it to me.

David Sexson: For teaching me about life, introducing me to Belisa, and being one of my best friends. Though you live far away and we no longer spend time together, you've impacted my life forever.

Travis Lively: For teaching, by example, what it means to be a man and a brother. Thank you for having the courage and loving me enough to call me out on my bullshit. The next cheeseburger is on me.

The SEAL community/military: When I entered the navy, I was a seventeen-year-old boy with big dreams and high expectations, and looking for a purpose in life. The navy is where I learned to be a man, to be a father, to provide for my family. The SEAL Teams is where I went looking for that one man to inspire me to say, "I want to be that guy," only to learn that there were many. I'm still that goofy teenage kid who thinks you guys are amazing and wants nothing more than to be just like you. This book gave me an opportunity to honor you and our heritage, and I hope it serves to attract more quality candidates to

BUD/S, so that you can hammer the shit out of them and make them quit. Thank you for pushing me past my limits and for teaching me the true meaning of brotherhood and that I can go farther than I ever thought possible. I carry you all with me every day. *Hooyah!*

Resources/Further Reading

Amen, Daniel G., M.D. *Change Your Brain, Change Your Life: The Breakthrough Program for Conquering Anxiety, Depression, Obsessiveness, Lack of Focus, Anger, and Memory Problems.* Revised and expanded edition. New York: Harmony Books, 2015. Also available as e-book.

Bassham, Lanny. *With Winning in Mind.* 3rd edition. Flower Mound, TX: Mental Management Systems, 2012. Also available as an e-book.

Blehm, Eric. *The Last Season.* New York: Harper Perennial, 2006. Also available as an e-book.

Csikszentmihalyi, Mihaly. *Flow.* New York: Harper & Row, 1990; rpt. New York: Harper Perennial Modern Classics, 2008. Also available as an e-book.

Fitzgerald, Matt. *Iron War: Dave Scott, Mark Allen, and the Greatest Race Ever Run.* Boulder, CO: Velo Press, 2011. Also available as an e-book.

Hardy, Darren. *The Compound Effect.* New York: Vanguard, 2010. Also available as an e-book.

Kipling, Rudyard. *Kim.* London: Macmillan, 1901. Also available as an e-book.

Medina, John. *Brain Rules.* Seattle: Pear Press, 2014. Also available as an e-book.

Pierson, Melissa Holbrook. *The Secret History of Kindness: Learning from How Dogs Learn.* New York: Norton, 2015. Also available as an e-book.

Pryor, Karen. *Don't Shoot the Dog: The New Art of Teaching and Training.* Revised edition. Lydney, Gloucestershire, UK: Ringpress, 2002.

Skinner, B. F. *The Behavior of Organisms.* New York: D. Appleton-Century, 1938; rpt. Boston: Copley Publishing, 1991.